THE BEST
AUSTRALIAN
POEMS
2 0 0 6

THE BEST
AUSTRALIAN
POEMS
2 0 0 6

Edited by

DOROTHY PORTER

Black Inc.

Published by Black Inc.,
an imprint of Schwartz Publishing

Level 5, 289 Flinders Lane
Melbourne Victoria 3000 Australia
email: enquiries@blackincbooks.com
http://www.blackincbooks.com

ISBN 186 395 2624

Printed in Australia by Griffin Press

Contents

Preface

Words move, music moves
Only in time: but that which is only living
Can only die. Words, after speech, reach
Into the silence.
—T.S. Eliot, 'Burnt Norton'

The last few years have been both fabulous and sad ones for Australian poetry. In memory of a number of recent deaths I have opened this new *Best Poems* anthology with a 'Prelude'. The poetry community, despite its reputation for petty squabbles and bitter feuds, is actually marvellously good at honouring its dead. Poets know how to do a wake. I've always felt that a poet's words, participating in an ancient, magical and incantatory tradition, keep that poet alive forever.

This book's 'Prelude', a brief memorial to five unique poets, gives a spicy sample of death, mystery, despair, politics, passion, language, place, ferality and subversion, one that is intended to prepare the way for the diversity of the poetry by living poets that follows.

I did not deliberately set out with a diversity agenda. I have a horror of the standard Royal Easter Show method and con – every child gets a prize. But it was impossible not to be impressed by and proud of the range and quality of recently published poetry collections.

Some of these books are outstanding. I hope that by showcasing them in this anthology, I will fire readers to hunt the books down for themselves. And buy them.

The real tragedy of Australian poetry is not how few good poets there are, but how few books of poetry are bought and read. It is wonderful to see the crowds hanging from the rafters at poetry gigs and to hear the roar as favourite poets perform their work. Poetry audiences are young, raucous and passionate. But poets do not live by applause alone. Our best books demand and deserve the same support by publishers, booksellers and readers that the alpha list of fiction and non-fiction takes for granted.

In reading for this anthology I was presented with an embarrassment of riches – from knuckle-raw elegies through pungent political satire to exquisite lyrical reflection and deft language play. I tried as much as possible to follow the motto, 'Without Fear or Favour', of 'Veritas', an incorruptible TV critic from my childhood. Doubtless I have missed some gems. My apologies to their authors.

My best, most memorable moments were the 'Eureka' ones, especially the discovery of a new poet in the unsolicited pile or in an obscure magazine. On the other hand there were also sobering surprises from poets whose work I had previously found deeply uncongenial.

I began reading through the boxes of books, magazines and loose poems with rigid resolution, thinking that I knew just what I was looking for. But I kept changing my mind. Finally, I just went with it and followed my nerve, as the contagiously relaxed New York poet Frank O'Hara once suggested. And my nerve jumped all over the place like a needle with a mind of its own, picking out intriguing tracks on a daunting vinyl record. (The iPod shuffle setting will never be as sexy a metaphor as a diamond needle.)

Perhaps in the end I was reading in the way I like to listen to new music. I wanted to be transported. I wanted to be delighted. I wanted to be changed. Not short-changed.

This is not a lukewarm anthology of Golden Oldies and Greatest Hits. From every poet there is a true and fresh note – even if on occasion an uncomfortably dissonant one.

My heartfelt thanks to all the poets.

Dorothy Porter
Melbourne, 2006

I.
Prelude

Prelude

The only space I've inhabited
has been my self.
Ask me where one street intersects
with another hereabouts
and I couldn't tell you.
Ask me their names and I'd say
Never heard of them.
I wouldn't exactly get lost
if you blindfolded and spun me
around three times a kilometre
from here. All I could say though
when the blindfold was taken off
and I was asked where I was
would be Manly.
Not the one I learnt by heart
as a child, or the other
I knew as a young man
its main street full of good
and varied shops.
It would be the one I call
the rotisserie with its
food shop souvenirs food shop
souvenirs all the way from the
wharf to Ocean Beach
in summer another kind of
rotisserie with the black coffee
coloured bodies and the bare
breasts inviting more than hot
stares. But that's the South
Steyne end we're in the section
somewhere back from that
portion of the lengthy beach

called North Steyne about its
middle flavoured by some
surfers and cultivators of
skincancers. It has plenty of
pleasant trees left pines figs
and gums most too old
and large for their own good.
But the only thing that shades Q'cliff
beach at 3pm is a 14 storey
block of units not a plot
of pines as they did 50
years ago. I was nearly
drowned there when I was sixteen
one year before the WW2's
ending. Sucked out and under
by a rip I was upheld
and tossed on a shoreward
wave by 2 young lifesavers
as true to their title as I was
to cowards. I never swam in
the waves again or body surfed.
That terrible stranglehold of
green coils and black depths
fascinated like a cosmic
anaconda from the distance
of the beach no closer.
I'd walk the shore to see
the women's bodies and watch their
minds trying to keep up
with them sexist and suicidal
at seventeen at nineteen
saved by a fate worse than
death by two of them
at loose ends with and without
husbands. By then a poet

but just as I didn't know
where I was geographically
I didn't know more than
four flowers from the others
three trees from the rest.
Reading Keats and Shakespeare
shamed as much as gave me joy.
I couldn't even tell what a piece of
cake tasted like. In fact
I avoided that word and the first
person singular almost from the
start. I fussed about with what
I saw and tried to reinvent it.
After writing about practically
nothing but love for several
years I tried to write about anything
but it for another 50.
But it squeezed itself
in and I know as much about it
as the streets trees flowers
ocean and all around me
that's next to nothing until I met
you and then I started oh
so slowly to set about
learning something of it
from you by you with you
and finally got it into
my system and out onto
paper once and for all
but even then it was over
30 years after the event
of events and of course
illegal in its intent
but by then I had learnt
to lose fears of that kind

and poured out my small amounts
of passion into thimblefuls
of additives to otherwise
almost impersonal poems
and finally before too
late opened what was left
of the floodgates rinsing
our landscape known
once and for all.

Bruce Beaver
1928–2004

On Re-reading Amis, Wain & Larkin

No more Movementese, please.
Take back all that very old
mouldy hat about tasteless
Common Sense in place of
passion fruit flowered Romanticism
Your Everyman's Castle isn't even
a home, it's a house where you
sit and sulk and play Bach
without really listening to
anything but the surface hiss
of the wear and tear of mundane
'reality', that unleavened dough
of things. Not very sustaining
even with an occasional radish
of sex crunched in, or that
embarrassing attempt at stomaching
an obligatory revolting and still
very fashionable steak tartare
of the underlying violence of
neighbours never yourselves no
you get it all out in cleverly stilted
but basically envenomed
verses and plaster of Paris prose
about the awful necessity of
the ordinary, the let's keep it
normal at all costs, even that of
too much sympathy and none at all
for yourselves all ingrowing
psychic toenails and incipient
mental ulcers. Plenty of brisk

nettle rubdowns, lots of cold
conclusions to come to. Reject
negate sift the dust of your
comfy mausoleums of
normalcy.
Nothing was ever intended to be
extraordinary. The exceptional automatically
is suspect. Anything that can't be measured
weighed and completely self-satisfiedly
categorised as useful in a wholly
functional fashion is out. So are you.

Bruce Beaver

nebuchadnezzar

from the paintings of arthur boyd
for sonny booth and lionel rose
in the voice of sonny booth

i am nebuchadnezzar
my balls are caught tight with white wire.
i am caught in extremis,
falling,
paying the price for the poor,
my body pays with fire,
for i am nebuchadnezzar, the king of fitzroy.
the clouds scud
and the subtle landscape of trees emanate from me
for i'm the king of what's loud.

i am nebuchadnezzar and I am the king of fitzroy,
my skin is black, my heart is strong
you see my gardens there in gertrude st
beneath the high rise flats,
that's my babylon,
the land that long i've fought for
on behalf of all my tribe
for this is my country and i am its king
whose balls are caught taut with white wire,
who sees blind on a starry night my gardens
whose peace is kept by police from the city of tyre
for i am nebuchadnezzar,
aflame i fall through fitzroy skies
(my diamond studded haven)

afire i fall into gertrude st
my fingernails become claws
and my hair to feathers forms.

for i am nebuchadnezzar
whose balls are still caught in the fire,
who goes to the brascoe for an eloquent piss
and find a hand, graffiti-ing the strange words,
'meme, meme, tekel, uparshin'
almost an indecipherable scrawl
etched lightly on the dunny's wall.

and on a saturday night in my kingdom of fitzroy,
wet with the dew of heaven,
i prowl with the lines through my parks,
grab lionel, he laughs,
he loves to congregate with lions –
such is lionel's spell.

for i am nebuchadnezzar
doing my time in the cells,
seven years in exile smoking lebanese gold
in that putrifying hell.
i have moved among the beasts,
stalked with them behind the forest of the bars
and on the starlit nights
have dwelt on savage dreams
while listening to murmurs from my beloved babylon.

for i am nebuchadnezzar
my heart has been stalled
by the fury of the streets of fitzroy,
the police are out with their batons
and my brothers have been felled in the gutters,
their black skulls are bleeding
the same blood that's on the lion's claws.

but i am nebuchadnezzar,
bastardry and beauty surround me
though i am still the king.
i dream a fitzroy tree
whose roots are deep in gertrude st,
whose shadow gives shelter to the beasts of the field

and the fowls of heaven find home along with my kin
for its leaves are as broad as the sun
for i am nebuchadnezzar, still the king of fitzroy,

still afire and falling
still blind on a starry night,
still dreaming the gardens of my beloved babylon.

Shelton Lea
1946–2005

Danger

imitated from the Sanskrit

Terrified, I watched
the leopards mating.
Inside the beauty of their skins
they thrashed, coupling.
Had I leapt
between them and tried
to yank them apart,
one mane in each hand,
I should have courted
far less danger
than that morning
in my skiff
when I stopped rowing
to watch you, poised
on the trunk of a dead tree
ready to dive
and set the river
on fire.

Richard Deutch
1944–2005

Midnight

My knees
can no longer hold me
as I crouch over
the grate,
hands stretched out to savour
the heat that is stored in
a deep pile of ash.

If I feed it
with scraps of kindling
a flame may start up,
flicker,
die down.

For how many years
have I tended this fire?
Now it will die
as all fires must die.

Though my hands are frozen
I still hold them out.

Vera Newsome
1912–2006

Matins, 1932

From the cliff top
I saw them
bent over
a rock pool –

four great, black,
white-wimpled birds.
Can these be birds?
No. Black-hooded nuns,

wading!
What innocent pleasure
enticed them
to tuck up their habits

and dabble in water,
like cockatoos
shrieking
at five in the morning?

Vera Newsome

To no one:
and Mary did time

Dear someone
out there who
may or may not
give a damn

'I'm not a liar
I'm not a thief'

But you don't give
a damn, don't
wanna get close,
worried it might
rub off, typical
welfare-cum-
social worker wanna
beeze

To whomever might
give me a passing
accidental glance,
to whomever might
have the guts to stop
and say hello

I didn't mean to
kill my baby daught
I wasn't right
I was sick

Dear anyone to anyone
who just might care
I didn't know
I just didn't know
I'm still not
sure

Lisa Bellear
1961–2006

II.

A Visitation

All night wild fire burned in the tree-tops
on the other side of the river – now
it's morning and smoking embers
from the angophoras are landing in a clearing
on the near shore. A yellow-footed rock
wallaby limps in from the bush,
dazed with mucked fur, its tail hardly able
to support its weight. Although
wounded, it seems miraculous
as the morning sun catches the yellow hue
of its feet above black claws.
It's the first yellow-footer I've seen for more
than forty years – and reminds me
of a time as a kid when I rowed
my grandfather's tallow-wood skiff across
Big Bay. There was a mob of four
rock wallabies, standing there as the boat
was pulled silently by the tide along
the shore. One I noticed, by the mottled fur
on its back, seemed to have mange,
like the river foxes of those days.
A panic suddenly ran through them
and the largest buck almost flew
straight up an enormous rock. It was sheer wildness,
so fierce it shocked me. Afterwards
the atmosphere was thick and I could smell
an odour unlike anything I recognised.
This morning, once again, that scent was in the air.
I turned to look but the wallaby had gone.

Robert Adamson

Appassionato

he thundered out! of a wild July | sweet
froth flicking from his steed's hot flesh
his hollering thrown like | punches to the
sky his mouth a noose-formed Munch!
I was a child when he first arrived | I
suppose you thought if he came at all
he would sneak up | stealthily! whisper
seductively! enshroud me | softly! in his
blanket of black but | No! it was always
violent & nights were worst with him
treading underground the possibility of
dream | dragging me heel-wise behind
his lead | promising providence but
giving me grief every second of every
day | *you / are / mine / yes / you / are /
mine* | he still visits me now | the same
old act | rearing above me practising
his art | pretending to | save! while
pulling me apart & the hooves those
hooves | hammering all over my heart ||

Jordie Albiston

Amoroso

the sea is a man | murmuring it gently
You are never alone | he calls me under
a lowering sky invites me | slyly! to
slip & slide | beneath his confetti of
ticker-tape foam | planets line | Up!
the axis lunges & Alaska falls right into
China | I crashed into love one day
like that & woke up a woman | alone |
the mountain is | male: he roars like
an iceberg on fire in the rain | shouting
out to me over his pain *Help me! Into
your heart!* | I melted myself one night
that way but | froze up quick smart
again when I saw | millions! charging
like moths love's flame | float by dead
the next morning | look | even the
poem is | masculine now: mouthing out
metaphors one by one | tongue in my
ear | hand on my thigh! arms astretch
in muscular lines | I am not inclined ||

Jordie Albiston

Lingo

He had the boat next to ours, and every morning I'd hear
his hammer banging quick repair upon a hank. None of us
went near him: he stank like an old fish trough; and rats –

white-eyed, snarly – nested in the frayed ends and tatters
of his coils of rope. Davey said he lived on deck among
rusted reels and old tackle, white-eyed as his rats, and

only went below to smoke and listen to his rusty cunner
pitch against the waves. We called him Lingo. On deck
he kept a cockatoo that he'd tried to teach to rip out oaths

in high Dutch and low German. The bird was old, and its
voice was as incessantly raucous as Lingo's thumb rasping
the milled silver edge of a lighter, when he'd put a flame

to one cigarette after another, cigarettes he'd roll between
his fingers, fine as patisserie dough. We'd hear him cough
over and over like a small hushed wave, the bird repeating

each fresh collapse. Despite the rats, the smell lifting
from his deck as if from the top of a gut-bucket, he never
fished or moved from his moorings. His left eye had

grown a cataract, grey and soiled as a mackerel scale; his
other was leaden, slitted, wedged in his face like a sinker.
Grennan would give him any eels he'd caught and he'd

string them up at the back of his boat like thick curtains
of bull kelp. People wanted him off the docks. We said
very little when they set the air ringing with rebuke.

One morning we heard a heavy, blunt bursting — and
found Lingo slamming the cockatoo into a pylon, cussing
like a rusted reel, his head long gone to his demons ...

Some mornings, when I hear the cold, undeniable wind
swing in from the silvered sea, I think of Lingo coughing
and swearing and moving the way his boat always did,

with a tilt to the right ... That cockatoo hardly ever got
his drunken words straight, but it could cough like a man
short-changing the air in his lungs with a smoke sixty

or seventy times a day ... I remember Lingo's face when
they chased him off: a mere nothing, a shape, an O
over which two dark eyes hung like a sorry umlaut.

Judith Beveridge

Jellyfish

Jellyfish, translucent as onionskin, pulse through the bay.
Davey gets one on his oar and lifts it up like a dripping
wad of plastic wrap. I see others floating in and out

of the shallows; changing colour like globes of thin
photosensitive glass. Later, when they're washed up
like old bait bags, kids will pierce them with sticks.

At least today the onshore wind isn't driving those
bluebottles in. Yesterday we scooped up a lot with
our oars and burst their gas-filled floats. Grennan

became angry, threw handfuls of sand on the coils.
He told us a bluebottle was not a single animal, but
a specialised colony. Then he dangled one of the long

fishing tentacles from his rod. It was as ragged
as a skein of unpicked knitting. Davey said later
he thought he was going to lash us with it, especially

when the veins in his neck and forehead turned blue
and knotted ... Davey lowers the jellyfish back into the bay,
a quivering mound of gelatin ... I think we can still

see Grennan's face and neck; that bulging circuitry of
veins; still feel his mouth venting words with about as
much sour air as we'd burst from those gas-filled floats.

Judith Beveridge

Still Life with Cockles and Shells

(Italian, c.17th; Kunsthistorisches Museum, Vienna)

Life breathes in this painting like a child
pretending not to be awake,

or a skink metamorphosed to a stone
but for the flutter in its flank.

You have to lean and listen for the heart
behind the shining paint,

the lips half-open, and the glittering eye.

Velvet of the night. A bald parrot on a parapet
watches to the east.

Ships listing on the waves
neither leave nor approach.

Someone has slain
five other birds: beaks, half-closed,

agonise in all directions.
A wash of unearthly light limes the sunken feathers.

What dreams the painter makes: I seem

to see inside the night
after Apocalypse,

when every soul has risen and sped off,
the violent seas at rest,

ships anchored and abandoned,
shells emptied of their monopods.

Or else the world has ended, but in
some other way;

and the parrot turns to give her
human greeting to the dawn.

Judith Bishop

Coffee

1.

there are a number of things I always liked about coffee

2.

drinking coffee alone I can enjoy reading Tony Towle
much more, or who*ever* I like

3.

one of the things I like most to do
is drink it standing at my door.
which leads out of the kitchen of our flat
& faces on the tin of the fence
3 feet away. above the tin
is the view. it is the city – something
else I like.

4.

drinking coffee out of a small cup which I like I enjoy
thinking about a problem of contemporary poetry: *too many
poets* like the word 'blue'.
I myself like it. – the sky
is that colour
& in the distance, against it,
the tallest buildings of the city are against it
or reach up into it cool-ly. Some cranes near some of them
do it too

5.
My coffee is finished

& I am lost in thought, leaning in the
open door.
the cat & I
are getting on quietly together.

            which is
no big deal. – neither of us wants to 'live' in

'The HAIKU'.

6.
the sky / is looking all
blue & 'oracular', hours before
a huge cloud was 'choiring' there, like a New Realist's
    version
of Tiepolo. both of them
tell me nothing. (that is, the sky being *blank & clear*,
& the cloud) the cat seems unaffected too.
I feel the way I hope Robert Motherwell might feel
– pagan, & immensely cultivated.

7.
as so often happens when I drink
coffee alone I don't think of anyone but myself

8.
the coffee has a bitter taste I turn my head to the left
as I change the foot I'm standing on
& down the path is a view between the two white, modern
    flats
of the water a narrow but terrific
                strip of it.
I feel terrific myself. the wind –
              which is moving it & making it
look like it is living is touching me. I like this particular
    contact
with the air &, indirectly, with the water –
              looking 'elemental' &
deep blue between the buildings
              – like Anthony Quinn
in the Mediterranean being
                    cliché

9.
I see him on a Greek isle in a little bayside
café, in the open   'Life' is bustling around, & even though
he has to do
      something important, he drinks his
small coffee
      & says – of the coffee – 'It is good'
& it is, it's terrific, coffee.

Ken Bolton

20/5/04

The television sets of my children
dispute space with each other.
Caught in the crossfire
I shelter like an artificial plant.
Whatever I plan slips away
beyond the edges of yesterday.
Buffeted by the winds of a great noise
I travel across black evening corridors
like the migration of some great thought from India
over enormous deserts to Alexandria
then by accidental telepathy to New York and Dublin.

Why was I sitting there reading a strange
interminable French novel on a train?
Why was it I never married you?
Between mismanagement and a culpable
fear of life I struggle on
to let yesterday bloom into the white fleeting dazzle
of railway station pickets passed at great speed.
With my pathological fear of the unknown
I stay behind dragging myself from washbasin to bed,
rocking myself into painlessness
on the shining floor
as vast and incomprehensible as the world.

Peter Boyle

Lost Soldier

The river was filled with bones
from the neighbourhood's family pets.
All sorts of bones: dog, cat, mouse.
There was even the dusty rib cage
of Mr Perkins, that old nag
the Irish twins saved from the knackery
and kept in their lounge room
on the tenth floor.
They used to bring Mr Perkins
down in the lift and ride him
along Seven Mile Beach.
No one remembered when
the bones started to collect.
Some say it was after the last rains.
No one can remember when
they were either. Sometimes
it almost seems ridiculous
that water could fall from the sky.
Mavis, the town's one-time spinster,
claims to have the last wet season
on video, but Joey found out
that was just a lure. One afternoon,
we pushed that dingbat Timmy
down the bank into the bones.
You could hear his big clumsy feet
cracking like fireworks
as a white cloud drifted up
wherever he went shrieking about.
He came back with the twisted vertebrae
of what looked like a big brown snake
or black snake, we couldn't tell which.

It reminded me of a book I'd read,
how during some war somewhere
they interrogated prisoners
by skinning them alive.
That riverbank made me think
there was a lost soldier in town
after a couple of answers.
I figured he lived under Brodie's place,
in the basement where Brodie's mum
kept the dressmaker's doll
and the family photos of the kid
that went missing.

Michael Brennan

One Hundred Nights

At the foot of the bed
the dog stirs.
You turn and settle.
All of us inch down further.
It is our hundredth night together.

Somewhere
a door slams,
footsteps
quicken on a pavement

somewhere
a branch
scrapes at a downpipe
in the dry wind

about us
a poor chorus
of draughts and wood-sound, stilts
sinking in the damp ground.

When will it end,
this waking
while others sleep,
this herding
out on the ghost fields?

the flesh
whispering
its impossible desires

the bones
murmuring their Kali mantra

love, emptiness
love, emptiness

David Brooks

David

Michelangelo's David is being restored by a 45-year-old single
woman who adores the eyes of David and has examined but
will not touch the genitals. 'Someone else will have to clean them.'
—Cinzia Parnigoni, quoted in the *Weekend Australian*, 14 February 2004

His flesh the last stone in his arsenal,
His white soul its own solid cloud of marble,
In his hair the dark globs of fallen wax
From those who covered him in candles
To see each detail of his form
The better to plug their hearts with this stone –

His manhood barely begun, his thoughts
Just now taking shape above his eyes
And in the crushing, passive hollow
Of his right hand that holds the future
Still and small as a bird –
His heart is a model prisoner
Ringing its harmless knuckles on his chest.

This moment loose, airy, unbalanced,
As if extinction will be nothing,
And no giant a match for these details –
She cleans 40 square centimetres a day,
Her solvent rag, her fingertips, her heart
Sending small shots of heat into the body of the boy.

And now she is near his left nipple,
His hand large enough to cup her head.
Each night the marble weighs
Against her sleep, its pits its cracks,
Its gaps filled with centuries of touch,
Black scum between his fingers:
He is a boy without a mother.

Each day his gaze is different for her –
All the thinking here belongs to him.
He is everything he appears to be.
His black eyes drilled into his own mind,
He dreams of lightning strikes and hammers,
Yes, and those who crawl over him
Unexpected, curious as rodents.

Under her hand each day he is still,
Vast with the future, endless as her own life;
She cannot imagine the giant above him
But must, for there is always a giant, for every child:
This lesson in memory, this boy waking
To his own son and love a form in air.
Her brushing touch a lover slowing time, this time.

Kevin Brophy

A Dictionary of Sentences

After being away from my son for a day his size frightens me.
Always I am surprised at the bitterness of coffee.
As she speaks I become aware of her breathing, and want to
   listen to this.
Even in prison, he said, I gave myself four weeks' annual leave.
He shows me his crippled wrist, the tattooed number on his
   arm, and a photo of his father, gassed.
I pedal for an hour and am half convinced I am going
   nowhere.
Like his grey shirt my colleague speaks of ethics as thing of
   doubt and compromise.
My Christian friend says it is all right to be without faith, for
   this is the most authentic condition for any Christian.
'Suddenly' my daughter's French sounds French (*tout à coup*).
The barking of the dog next door is always expressed as a
   question.
The motor mower has one thing to say and like knowledge it
   fills the head briefly.
The nearest I can come to conversion is to begin each day
   immersed in water.
The visit: pointing to a chair he closes the door.
This novel, she says, is too wordy (and I want to tell her it is
   the words that I love).
When a man's beard is that luxurious it becomes impossible
   to listen to what he says.
We speak of the weather because in truth it tells what is
   within us.

Kevin Brophy

To a City

To a city where I'll remember nothing
But a clump of yachts
Stuffed like nénuphar in every tiny inlet
To the heart of the world's palladium
To the sky coloured excessively
So sky-blue over Shark Bay
All your red-eye filters can't protect your citizens
My poetry is exposed in a dazzling glare
The notebook's white page is blinding
My tomato-pink cheeks are pricking
Goodbye Sydney
I'm tired of your multi-coloured rosellas
Fruit bats and cockatoos.
Except for the Greens
I'm weary of your politics too.
The immigrants
Are fed up with your cockroaches
And scurrying rats
Farewell blood-smudged pillow slip
My war against mosquitos won
Now, no one will say 'worlds collide'
The plane takes off
Your horizon morphs into a blurred outline
Off-register in magenta, cyan and yellow

(my Cendrars)

                                    Pam Brown

Withdrawal

the librarian looks like Barbie on
stiletto heels hair spiked in auburn silver
and magenta over tiny face possum eyes behind
batwing glasses a name like a beauty salon
behind her on a desk small pelts
protected in plastic bags or maybe
Bill Oddie's sporrans plotting escape
laughing at the Goodies is a long way
from the fluorescence of the oncology
unit as the lights shimmer
on rainy streets outside
Barbie frowns as she tucks floating
strands into an Ena Sharples net
can she remember Coronation Street
pulls a dead animal over her client's
skull pushing a multi-frown
wave fashion down her forehead
combs the springy synthesis
tweaks with perfumed dedication
raises an eyebrow in question
at the grim stranger in the mirror
who is unconvinced insists they try
another this time she is a '60s Cilla Black
no one will know it's me she cries
that could be a good thing the librarian replies
and pulls out a silver highland terrier
with bouncing curls a gleam of corrective
zeal in her magnified eye

a withdrawal is made taken away in a bag
with comb and shampoo she'd like to
release it into the wild but she's promised
to return it when her own hair grows back
even so she can see her wig scurrying down
the drain to hide for as long as it takes

Anna Buck

knochentrocken

the guitar played on
in the food court like
a tooth recently distracted
the blockbuster movie demolished
the adjoining church before the
congregation had time to read or forgive
the credits another normal saturday at the used
car yard where the chimera keened for the quietude
of the resurrected desert, the libretto highway riddled
with the bacteria of entertainment, everyone licking at
icecream like fury in pyjamas, the random jury eulogising
the attractiveness of syrup colour at the launch of the
charitable donation pancake, the digital dog sniffing through
its plasma for the sound of a deliciously smelly bone

joanne burns

written in the bath/Irish colophon*

Death is embarrassing
as greed – rushing

into the long stare
at an ancient page

like a ball into the reflex of the hand
the stars hurtle in

from the margins
of the straightened room – racked by error

made rigid by terror of it
you shiver

the shiver of the sunburnt the shell
emptied by the sea

and again by the pressed ear
History

is the highest paranoia
you only can ever just be yourself

your head
under the water your heart

in your ears the sound of footsteps
retreating – *three fingers only*

are writing – the whole body
is in agony

Elizabeth Campbell

---

* colophon: marginal graffito. The words italicised are from an Irish MS
of the 9th century.

Letter to Walt Whitman
re: Iraq

If you were there now,
you'd lie down with those
who struggle on the ground
like half squashed worms,
down with the maimed,
misused, disowned.

If you were there now,
you'd kneel, importunate,
give yourself to silence, mutely
cradle the stomach-blown
villager.

James Charlton

Blue-Tongue

Fat like a full tube
of toothpaste

it freestyles past
the boulders dropped
by our lemon tree

sets fire
to dead leaves
and imitates a rock
abysmally

Aidan Coleman

Dragons

for Bobby

There must be a deep need for them
for although Nature in all her experiments
never got round to dragons,
there they are:

winged like fruit bats, serpent-scaled,
cats'-eyed, owl-wise,
and talking in parrot-tongues,
but most of all imbued with human breath
capable of razing forests,
turning ice mountains to melt-water
and making deserts from ungulate savannahs.

They are us:
virgin hungry,
solitary but necessarily social,
full of mysterious destiny,
but never fully in control.

They are our other:
extinct, before they're born.

Julian Croft

Foxglove (Digitalis)

for Hilary Astor & Imelda Dodds

Stop my heart!
The cup of close-drawn flowers
is drinking me
in a suburban backyard.
Why haven't I seen you
for this long long time
and yet your welcome is four-door: a morsel,
a drink, a chair, and all those
warnings about poison?
Why did we stop sharing screams
counting on our youth
deep into the body's sour night?
I am sure we walked over that grass
and up that street.
Do you know I still dream about you,
recalling your face in the dark
and as it should it offers no excuses
for my obsession
yet again and again stops me here
in the recollection.
And after the heat has died
I want to pick out your bones
from the ash of my heart;
to eat the flower
they tell me not to eat.

M.T.C. Cronin

Why Liberation from Dictatorship May Take Some Time

Our Great and Fearless Leader
(may His Name be forever praised!)
like a wise farmer has planted
many fields full of ears

In the particles of dust
from the sandstorms
He is also present; if we would breathe
we must do so very carefully

In those distant clouds
in the heavens above us
hidden cameras record
our every activity

Even the birds on the city rooftops
as well as those in the distant villages
cock beady eyes and fly swiftly
to inform Him of all that we say

Now foreigners come, bearing (they tell us) freedom
– but freedom is only a word we have heard
fluttering like a feather on the lips
of the dying

Bruce Dawe

Divining Colander

for A.T.B.

The kitchen vessels that sustained
Your printed books, my poems, our life,
Are fallen away. The words remain –
Not all – but those of style and worth.

And here, in Age, I feel the need
Of some Divining Colander
To hold the best of all since done
And let the rest slip through.

Rosemary Dobson

Fantasia on a Theme
by T.S. Eliot

I saw a vision of the street
that would confuse the street
a politician's underpants
an aerogram from Paris, France
an invitation to the dance
(a balcony seat)

blow your nose, expectorate,
the world is filled with doctorates
waiting in the mist for a bus

★

The winter evening settles down
like a failed soufflé
a television glow
announces more than we'll ever know
a play-within-a-play
evokes from its auditor a frown

★

Because I do not hope to think again …

★

Shall I dare to eat a Porsche?

Laurie Duggan

Golden Coast

Adrift on the highest floor of this hotel,
I gaze beyond, around, between the boast
Of all the glassy towers which make their mark,
Their ulceration of the golden coast
Whose beauties they would sell,
Under the settling sediment of dark.

The miles of curving beach fade to the south
From where the lights as laggardly as sound
Struggle to make the passage of the gloom.
A plane's red beacon floats towards the ground.
You turn and kiss my mouth
And draw me from the evening to the room.

They say the end might come with little warning,
The climate breaking and the ecosystem
Collapsing almost overnight to pay us
The recompense of our belated wisdom,
Presenting in the morning
The advent and the only light of chaos.

Now, looking out with you held in my arms,
I see the buildings really are of glass,
Seen through and seen away with no more trace
Than last night's waves, the way cloudshadows pass,
The coastline's golden charms
Naked to view as you in my embrace,

Mapped and swept clear below us as my eyes
And hands explore your body's golden coast.
This day unknown to time will be there when
The light drifts through the shallows like a ghost
And dies of hours, the skies
And earth fall down and chaos comes again.

Stephen Edgar

Do You Copy?

Yes, I hear you. I hear
something else too.

Litter, I suspect. Let it brush
against you as you blow

down the street – you'll
soon find out how sticky things
can get when you
really stop
concentrating.

I stopped copulating
ears ago. These days the only
f. twinges I forget are forced
metaphors. Ah, here's
an example.

This one's me, kiddo. It was taken
someplace no one went to
and was, they told me,
dribblingly attractive. Do I
believe this? What do you think?

I relieve no one, sir, for less
than a hundred dolours.

You do it for me though.
Exactly.

Chris Edwards

The Ibis Grove

Riverside, six Monterey cypresses
rise from a garden, their wolf-ear tufts thatching
a tenement of branches. Each evening,
ibis fly in: as they settle, an opera of
hooked rasps and drawn-out croaks till night comes down.
From the pier I watch an estuary
flat as a tarn but for the poetry of
surface tension embossing a white sky,
the drowned green tower reaching towards me.
Beneath it, later, the coming dusk
already inside that creepered cavern,
I hear the wind-crack and jarred groan of a ship
tacking beneath clouds the stained white of
ibis plumage, miming their dusty cries.

Diane Fahey

bagboy

he knew the butt tattoo his friend had but said nothing
afraid someone might think theyd swum together in the
    school of
easy knocks or aversions he came like a shark & butted
his teeth into the lovers they locked him in a cell
the bays connected to the sea like a heart & he
had rather kill than retreat to his midden of pipis
noone writes about it noone has the rough knife on bark
style needed at night when the nausea peaks & his work
lies undone & an automatic feeling brings him close to
    someone
who says what he auditions to the air & the speeding
trees he empties his pockets as pathetically as at an airport
sunshine you arent going anywhere but theres noone there
    to say
it only a building sensation & blood coming out of him
in ecstasy or as close as hell get sympathetic homicide they
call it hallucinatory bullet wounds & the culture says
    adulterys anachronistic
& jealousys for straights it seemed to him hed proven
    something
the prison had great acoustics & he had an escapees lungs

Michael Farrell

The Poet's Sister

The unseen birds singing in the mist
—Dorothy Wordsworth's journal

You were almost an unseen bird yourself,
singing your songs for a privileged few,
eager-eyed, always walking,
noting everything you saw – fields
and fells and shining rocks – when
you were not starching linen,
mending clothes or baking pies,
grilling a chop for Coleridge – to eat in bed;
copying your brother's verse,
or lying in the orchard on the grass,
you and William, looking at sky through leaves
and listening to the ceaseless sound
of water falling down the mountain.

Reading your journal, I marvel too
at everything you saw. That solitary leaf
blown like a rag in the wind,
still clinging to the tree,
mosses you gathered in the woods,
a beggar child in once-fine shoes,
and sheep reflected in the lake,
so still it was. On you walked,
in moonlight, sunshine, snow,
autumn mists, winter winds and sleet,
you and beloved William, he so prone
to sleeplessness and headache,
and you, scarcely robust, yet together
pressing on through showers,
regardless.

I think you saw them first,
those hosts of golden daffodils
dancing on that sombre day,
when the lake was dark and rough,
and his idea of wandering
lonely as a cloud was fanciful
to say the least. *You were both there;*
you wrote it down so freshly,
while he composed
a little fib.

Barbara Fisher

A Relationship with Fear

Fear sits in the front row and heckles when you speak in public.
   Fear loiters around the train station at night.
      Fear joins you on a long flight
  and annoys you with nervous chatter.
Fear walks into a crowded room at the same time as you,
    and you discover mutual interests.
       Fear doesn't believe in coincidence, and neither do you.
   Feeling more comfortable with fear than with others,
you start spending time together.
   Fear listens during the long and lonely hours,
      sharing quiet moments while the city sleeps.
  Before long, you're using the language of 'us' and 'them'
and finishing each other's sentences.
   Though there's conflict, you can't bear to be apart.
     So fear moves in for good.
   Gradually, you start to see another side of fear.
After a few drinks one night, fear becomes aggressive
   and puts you down in front of others.
     Fear hangs around the house all day,
  wanting to know your movements.
Jealous of you going out with friends,
    fear confronts you in a dark alley of the mind,
      saying the world is dangerous,
   but the 'unknown' is worse.
Fear tells you that government policy makes sense,
   that razor wire should be everywhere.
     You express a need for space,
  but fear says you can't cope on your own.

One day fear locks all the doors and won't let you out of the house.

One day you come home and find fear curled in a foetal position.

One day fear disappears and doesn't return for months. You hear a rumour that fear has found someone else.

Then one day fear arrives at your doorstep, begging to be let back in.

Cameron Fuller

chair pose

the mothering sky
bloods my eyelids, burns a hole
the size of a prayer.

palms pressed in forget, déjà-
vu the drug of choice.
and was it you that cut or

me that tore the gauze?
skeins of clouds go believing,
unmaking themselves

Kevin Gillam

In Praise of Mania

If for you the universe blazes
like the biggest Catherine wheel ever pinned
to a paling fence, and you rush to tell us about it,
it means you are chosen, not doomed.

If you drive your Mini like Ben Hur,
babble of chariots when the police turn up
and dance in the dark of a paddy wagon,
it means you are saved, not infected.

The world isn't apples, it's snakes,
no move is really the right one,
and the Lord loves those who have a go
more than all of his cautious angels.

And the blessed who see no risk
at all, but rush like saints
straight to the heart of disaster, and get there
ahead of the rest, are his special favourites.

They sing with Him in the burning bush,
they glow like Tilley mantles
and collapse into ash at a poke
of his Finger. They are always remembered.

Ross Gillett

In Thought They Lived Like Russians

They stripped the furniture from their flat,
and put on gloves to pay the rent,
they scorned their freeholds in the fat
    of middle class content,
lived like a tightrope walking act,
like a minimalist's artefact.

Sustained on bubbly and distress
and austere single-mindedness,
they probed extremity's milk-blue vein,
yet their attuned unhappiness
    was prudent not to waste.
no not the effervescent least
of their virtual champagne.
They were the fate within the novel,
where joy and disenchantment join
at some not altogether sane
    not altogether pain-
        -ful level.

Alan Gould

Fireplace

Rolled-up newspaper balls,
    like discarded drafts
of letters which overflow the wastebasket,
    are placed on the bricks,
and then you weave
    a version of that basket,
at first out of twigs
    and then with ever larger sticks,

before touching a match
    to the structure's foundation
and watching for flame
    to spread like cruel rumours.
Soon the iron grate
    is under occupation
from an upward-flowing
    river of heat. Its humours

while it devours the earth,
    air and moisture which adhere
to the logs you bring in
    from the shed are changeable
as the moods
    of any tyrant; it will spare
mere splinters while reducing
    broad beams to ash. Able

to seem like a living
        entity – the ancients
thought that life itself
        was a flame, forever
burning inside us – in fact
        it is death sentient
between the hearthstones.
        Shapes appear: a feather

and a swaying kelp-bed,
        a row of sirloin
steaks in a butcher's window,
        faces with glowing eyes,
a ruined chimney-stack
        in a pasture of red stone,
the lights of a distant city
        under fog, skies

at sunset, pyramids and plateaus,
        and at last a heart
pulsating ever more feebly.
        It all dissolves
into a fine white dust,
        so in the morning the hearth
could be a vacant landscape
        under snow. The world revolves

outside, as you watch,
    unable to turn away
from the fitful glow
    of the last declining coals;
it feels as though
    you are sitting, compelled to stay
at the bedside of a fading relative,
    while the hospital's

lights are turned down,
    and shadows like floodwater
rise in corridors.
    The last feeble spark
gives out, and you are left
    alone; but then a daughter
cries out in her sleep,
    somewhere else in the dark.

Jamie Grant

Wing-Beat

In some last inventory, I'll have lost a season
through the occlusion
of summer by another hemisphere.
Going there
the winter tolls twice
across the year. The leaves of ice
in their manuscripts
are shelved on the air and each sifts
fine as paper-cuts along the wind. I will go
to crippled snow
moving through the crossings, in the headlights
of early nights.
How glorious summer is to them
who have caught just a glimpse of its billowing hem.
'Fifty springs are little room,' an authority
in loss warns, but actuarially
I can expect to own
ten summers, before the heights of blue close down.
Although I've gone
northwards, I shall cross the lawn
at home – the trees and yard in bloom –
in the mirror in an empty room.

Robert Gray

Somewhere on the Shelves

The first floor of the library
is a warm juggernaut of books
pushing north
in the worst April storm for decades.

The last window is a blear of leaves and rain
and there is no such thing as distance,
where I am bound in the journal collection
reading old editions of the *TLS*. And

here's a poem entitled *Reading in the Library*
I might have written had I been someone else
somewhere else. Like mine it deals with time
and place but not the ephemeral

curling of a page
nor the blanch of pen and ink.
I scan it a second time
as if it were a draft of mine:

a midwinter weekend at Margate Sands
each hour constructing an unthinkable fence
of wind and rain it would be impossible
to climb back from –

and what was broken irreparably
anyway, afterwards. As with a tendency of mine
I notice too many adjectives upon the noun
as if one could never be sufficient

for the construct of metaphor and meaning.
Outside the windows the hour is sinking
in cold dark waves of afternoon.
The newspaper pages are reflected in a damp blur

of light and the poem again settles as in a skittish
shower of strange droplets
giving a precipitate shape to words
before the first signs of wreckage.

Jeff Guess

From *The Kindly Ones*

Kristin leaves me alone with Jade.
Wrapped in second-rate motel reality –
drambuie and videos in the afternoon –
sudden violent fucking, biting,
the kind of fucking you do after days of fucking

the muscles loosened by alcohol
desire tightened, the rooms available neon
and the reflection of chrome on the cars
outside the hot sun
air that at dusk smells sweet

Jade drives me out of town, past her old place.
Waves her hand out the window:
I lived in behind that hill, she says, then, speeding away,
I smell the wind just before we're stopped
by the police: twenty over the limit.

Back in the Isis café, we read leaflets about
birdlife in the swampland opposite
where the gazebo in the lagoon beckons in sunset light.
I eat her toast, and pick up
the Sydney paper from two days ago:

an article about an Australian doctor
who has discovered
that the clitoris is in fact
about seven inches long, extending
inside the muscle wall

This explains quite a lot, I said
passing the paper over to the others
Not enough studies were done
on women's anatomy, the doctor said,
or what existed was inaccurate

If medical textbooks showed the look of the vulva
at different points of excitation, as a series, it would
make more sense. Then if they could show the soul trying
to re-establish itself, its degrees of transformation
becoming a goat –

realising the nonsense of that –
becoming a human, swilling and rutting as if
that was all humans were good for,
or creating long oral histories
about swillers and rutters

The Circe the swine the swillers of wine,
the hill fort, the pleasure dome
the anatomy of all geography
the fact that travelling is so often about sex,
breaking rules, being somebody else.

The body of the lover, nibbled at,
made noble, adored, deified –
sometimes I thought
it contracts to a shudder that clenches
the whole understanding.

After, the mind roams in deep space
so the identity is stretched to a no-point.
It's a mild autumn night – I turn on Beck's radio –
another solar system has been discovered:
it has seventeen planets so far

We have realised planet formation is common.
The motel owner knocks and puts her head in the door.
Girls? Someone here called Tisiphone?
I lift my hand. The message is, she says,
Your sisters have gone home for a while.

The radio goes on: information has come back
from a space capsule launched in the 1970s
and which is now eleven billion k's away.
However it would have to travel for another 300,000 years
to actually get to Epsilon Andromedae.

Epsilon Andromedae is almost certainly not
the only other solar system in the galaxy.
I cut a pomegranate and put the seeds
on Jade's tongue. Her laptop looks like a lolly.
I begin to kiss a runnel in her left ear.

The desire for solitude watches the desire for sex
break through, have its way –
solitude rebuilds the fort wall
even as the vaginal wall subsides to its normal shape
and we breathe out

Solitude tries to extricate itself
from creation and just be quiet –
I walk around the town – bat-winged, god-eyed.
Sulphur-cresteds & currawongs
are eating all the fruit.

Without thinking about it
I become a bird and eat you
Jesus, the fruit of Mary's womb –
I try your succulent body
for my bread and wine.

On the last night of my holiday
we play Twenty-One for hours. The girls ask
where I'm going, and I hold up the joker:
a kookaburra with a snake in its mouth.
I'll be back, I say.

Jade presses me. I say I may have to go into hell
for a while, and she backs off, decides
I'm making reference to something private.
She looks at my mouth again
I have that feeling of the branches

of my nerve ends blossoming.
Careless, falling in love with a mortal,
the kind of thing you do on holiday,
or as a form of respite from your life
your miserable punishing life –

For days, I walk. There's a Drought Summit
in Parkes, but I don't got there.
I board a Greyhound south and head
for the Bush Races Festival at Gundaroo
and wander in the dust past the stalls –

the whip-maker, the man who makes harps,
the gem merchant with his displays of smoky quartz.
At the dog-jump we laugh at the plucky
Jack Russells leaping
onto the back of the ute.

I miss my sisters. If I go to hell
and stay there I'll never live with Jade,
I'll live in a place whose reigning ethic
is punishment, and that place is hell,
circular as its own argument.

If I stay above ground and lose my solitude
in gaining a wife, will I not risk
losing her to something as ridiculous as
snakebite on her wedding day?
Keep your shoes on, girls.

Susan Hampton

Hand, Chainsaw and Head

Mortlake Buskers' Festival

He juggles a chainsaw, a rubber hand and plastic head
the ghoulish toys of Quake's dark alphabet – Widow Maker,
Skull Splitter, Brain Biter – old Nordic weapons – their names

too, might find a place in his Mortlake armoury. The day
is sodden, and grey – even the fine patinating rain
feels like sprayed blood on my face and lips. The children

are bored and wish they hadn't come, but when he kick-starts
the chainsaw, they sense the danger of an R-rated thrill.
We're afraid he'll slip and fall on the wet road

but he juggles his macabre salad well, measuring
the saw's jittering arc between eye and wrist, and I admire
the steadiness of his touch as the children become bored even
    by this.

Returning to Melbourne, they sleep in the back of the car.
The sky falls thick as silk across the windscreen, and over the
    sound
of wipers and tyres I hear the wind's faint carousing
    polyphony.

A star drags the ceiling of a cloud. Now and then
houses eulogise the emptiness. The radio crackles and fades
as laden lorries sweep past like mescaline thunder.

The gossip of a child asleep is beautiful, I think,
but where to place ghosts, ghouls and opiate séances –
corpses and the whiskey games of death?

I juggle a machine, the mist and the night – the road thinner
darker than before – danger ahead, out of sight.
Wanting to be entertained, the landscape leans in – watching.

Jennifer Harrison

Changzhuo's Bees

Here is a photograph of Changzhuo, the Chinese apiarist
who sculpts with bees, who tucks the queen under his chin

calling the swarm to his face, the workers settling into the shape
of his mouth, nose, brow, until he has a mask of bees

and the stillness of marble or ice. Imagine the vibrato
of his chest; how he must delve into his breath, until

it is the breeze of the flower tipped over by dew.
Pollen and hive – the dizziness.

Pietà of bees – he is motionless as a pixilated mother
looking down at the first tug on her breast –

does she, too, exhale? Yet Changzhuo looks up
so as not to trap the bees between his chin and chest –

the gesture armours him as the word mother can.
Summer's sublime lavender store? A shell finding form?

Here is a son's school project on Virudunagar
and here's a daughter's violin, its dusty case full

of her scratchy wings. Here are kindergarten art works
locks of floss-soft hair in a grandfather's collar-box.

Here are beloved masks, gathered as discarded.
Breath of the bee, what needs have shaped me?

The swarm must have lifted from Changzhuo's face but I
    haven't
yet seen a picture of that. Was he unscathed, always?

Jennifer Harrison

Spiders

I stare from my study window into trees.
Considering all things, I watch the first snow spill
White seeds across the rubble where the barn
Towered over us with its cracked spire
For almost half a century until
Some feckless pot-head changed
The whole thing into fire.

Considering all things and their seasons,
Last night I rose to call you, full of delight:
Can we dine together, tonight or any night?
Candles, glasses, I had the whole thing framed
And zoomed. Then stopped. The toad of doubt
Filled the room. Everything swung about
Half-circle. I think it won't swing back.
I have my reasons.

Your husband hated my bones. Dead
Ten years, the slightest thought of him can goad
Me backwards into anger. The way he carked *Not so!*
Or fingered the thin fuzz on his weasel head
When bested in an argument, the dumb
Weight of his scholarship that hung
Like bags of fool's gold under his eyes.
Casaubon in the desert: a dried-up tarn.
Round him nothing flowed.

Should I dine with you tonight, or any night,
He will invite himself, sour ghost.
He'll spread his elbows everywhere. The toast
Will turn to wood-chips, the vol-au-vent
Spawn spiders who'll multiply and starve
The evening with their hairy eyes.
They'll clog our mouths with silence.

Dead or alive.
We carry our spouses everywhere.
They cling to us like varnish to a chair.
For many years, a liminal man, I've loved
You well, the way you moved
Round difficult things so lightly, lightly –
And found an elegant thing to do
Or say, while I – correct and diffident –
Admired, and told no one at all,
Not even you.

The blade of prudence has a double edge, *e verro?*
It can turn around and spike you like an arrow.

And even while our varnish chips and cracks
It's still the same:
His breath will smother every flame
And you will hurry off and rub your hand
Across the chilled vinyl of his bucket-seat
And flick the radio and drive off fast
While a saxophone blares
Across black snowdrifts – all three of us
Separate now, disaffection rising
To mingle with the stars.

Keith Harrison

Plum Trees

What the plum trees were doing
was loading galaxies of flowers
like night sky's sprawling fire
in the middle of daylight.

Space turned into bloom and fruit.
Soil rose into juice and scent.
Electric, shaken, utterly still,
unpruned wands thirsted for Spring.

Like gluttons, the trees sucked everywhere
from hidden water, seemingly nowhere –
that was the ground inside the dark
as we walked dry earth, dead grass.

Unreasonably, not beyond forgetting,
it's that year's dry light which falls away
as if plum trees flare in unfenced shadow,
momentary as thought, or as a trace of thought.

Martin Harrison

West of Al Shualla*

from Peter Henry Lepus, in 'Iraq, 2003'

Are all Arabs Muslims? Peter Henry asks.
Nobody answers him.
*She's got dark hair that stops
just above her shoulders. Turns up at the ends.
She's very slim,* Max says.
He's talking to Hamid
about Weasel Smith's girlfriend,
whom he is hoping to meet
somewhere south of Baghdad.

Do you have a wife in Australia? Hamid
politely asks.
Max snorts, Peter thinks, like one
of Hamid's camels. Then, less rudely,
I'm not married, Max says, *though I might
if it works out with Braid.*
Looking from one
to the other, they are sitting on same-size camels,
Peter sees Hamid
looks much bigger
          & taller
                than Max;
                      he remembers
his mother's puzzled recall
of an oral lore,
                passed down
from unknowable rabbits,
                      living
                          perhaps centuries
                                before:

It is not polite
to be rude to those
                    who are
                        larger
                            than oneself.
He remembers, too, that,
though she kicked with extreme ferocity,
when tunnelling earth,
& could, in adversarial conversations,
be vigorous, as well as firm,
she'd not been rude to anyone.

Peter has been studying his notebook,
somewhat awkwardly, from the back
of the third camel. Clifta – minus her cargo pants –
is hiding under the pommel. He has noticed,
since she's grown a little taller,
they have not fitted her well.

There is a dead Iraqi
wrapped in Max's plastic ground sheet
roped stiffly to the camel's side.

J.S. Harry

---

* Al Shualla – a fictional location that may or may not relate to an actual
   one which is spelled differently.
   Clifta is a junior Huntsman Spider who has been travelling for some
   time with Peter Henry in Iraq.

Strange Tractors

It's an ancient method of
ploughing—more ancient even that
boustrophedon—two cattle retracing
their steps in parallel lines

No, here there's not a
straight line to be seen anywhere—chaos
in the shape of two vulval wings—
the butterfly effect

Susan Hawthorne

Homecoming

You land with gold over the Red Centre still in your head.
The road taking you home to the sea is a lizard flattened in
    the heat.
The light does the talking, the light splinters all over the place.

Who lives here? Who comes into the leaf-lit room?
An ancient traveller is led by a warm lovely hand into a garden.
Look, look, look, says blessedness, before he eats and sleeps.

One bird then another bird keeps him afloat and awake –
lillypond mind, the lapping of silence, old waters that are deep,
a sleep at the bottom of the ocean, sleep drowning memory.

Later the same day that is night he wakes into silence.
There, nearby and faraway are the loved ones speaking,
the right words in their throat, cooing into his speechlessness.

Later the same day it seems to be the real sea he is in,
salting the odd word, washing him back into blazes of time.
Rediscovering his freestyle under the Turneresque bushfire sky

he swims – that's it, you swam into the aesthetic of home-
    coming!
They have not changed they are only more beautiful your
    loved ones.
You kiss the return, you find specks of ash on the pillow.

Barry Hill

Double or Quits

Sydney, 2006

One when we are under different skies
The truth strikes home of what love has become:
A compact it takes time to realise
Is better far, being less burdensome,
Than that first tempest by which we were torn.
Tonight you're there, where both of us now live,
And I am here, where both of us were born,
But there is no division we need give
A thought to, beyond localised regret:
For we will be together again soon,
And both see the one sunrise and sunset
And the face saved and the face lost by the moon –
The clouds permitting, which they seldom do
In England, but at least I'll be with you.

I'll be with you from now on to the end
If you say so. Should you choose otherwise
Then I will be a jealous loving friend
To wish you well yet prove it never dies,
Desire. Your beauty still bewilders me
Though half a century has passed. I still
Stand breathless at the grace of what I see:
More so than ever, now the dead leaves fill
The garden. A long distance will soon come.
Today, no. Nor tomorrow. But it must
Open the door into Elysium
For one of us, and me the first, I trust.
May we stay joined, as these two sonnets are –
That meet, and are apart, but just so far.

Clive James

The Library in the Snow

The library in the snow sleeps under a drift of frozen
words deep in its white landscape
the library steps are hard beneath the roof line

where first pale light drips from lattices
you have come here to browse
the text of storms, where shivers in a winter sun

melt back, mere shards of air
you have come to borrow something from this pock
of drops pattering down that all dissolves, is dissolving

as you enter, blue lightning seeps in the intricate sleep
of white trillions, turning sills to ice
chill filigrees of chance, weightless galaxies

float beyond your index here
still, no microscopic slice of infinity
duplicates, as texts in the library in the snow

are crystalline, where alphabets pile up
pale fires in leaping fractals and frozen spiral
dance, so run your finger down these brittle spines

crazed with bright ice, insignia, whorls, crisps
consult coins of five to seven, then twelve sides spinning
into circles spun of lattice logic, from each point anew

new fabric bursts from frost-webbed fire
read each shield, crested with its numbers here
where words extend pure petals of mathematics

their phrases are arrayed in snowy glyphs
and lines make light of radiant craters
where whole books float down to you

cold-drift and silence softly falls across the roof
underneath the whirling world outside
read on, before you become absorbed

completely in yourself
read on, before fingerprints fuse
and splinter into one cold cosmos

then turn from these steps
turn from the library in the snow
leaving with your borrowed time

your spiral key, your pentagram
your radial web, your bright helix
your wheel, your annulus, your star

John Jenkins

The Photographer Francis Bacon and Sylvia Plath Stalk Big Game in Equatorial Africa

His camera on its tripod has captured her interest.
It reminds her of her bee box. The Savannah reeks and
   clammers

all around them. He's telling a story and he's the hero:
The rhino approached full pelt. The camera had to be swung

which accounts for the blurred grass in the photograph.
She feels the weight of it; this midget's coffin. Puts her eye

to the little grid and at first finds it dark with the swarmy feel
of African hands. The vista opens when she takes off

the lens cap. Grass with a razor's edge. Pancake trees
as if a fairytale god had flattened them with a boot.

A giraffe manages the distance on its circus stilts while
he explains his obsession: *It's like I stop the feral beat*

inside me dead in the instant of the click. She straightens up
knowing he's wasting his time. The shutter will never

move fast enough to catch what's in him,
no matter how he see-saws the camera. Remembering

those two times she tried to kill the endless buzz in her head,
to overexpose her familiar maniacs, tip them belly-up and out

like fuzzy gold coins from a timber skull. Only to find
quicker than she could have imagined, the sticky

hive of survival trapping her while workers
turned their barrel bodies in the solitary confinement

of each hexagonal cell. No finger on the button.
All vision, no viewfinder.

And her ego just a rumble on the grass outside, a beast
in the act of charging.

Judy Johnson

Waking Alone by the Radio

I am recovering from too much
drinking or dreaming
you're phoning from up-country
with woes of a drowned camera
(corrosion, insurance and bruises).
Yet you can visit frozen cobwebs
around the veranda.

Morning radio trickles in its woes and strangers
a little piece of sky burnt bright
as it fell over Sydney this morning.
Listen to the astronomers explain!
Then there's the world
all the contusions we know and don't know
my knee or my dream is stiff where it clipped the floor.

You tell me that down by the creek
there were twelve baby platypus, with bright eyes
they are curious you say
and no bigger than your hand.

Jill Jones

A Luminous Tortoise Near Muswellbrook

Approaching Muswellbrook, a city with a name promising
sinuous organisms
in a watery expanse the early settlers must have brought
whole, in their minds, from England

suddenly on the bitumen I see this tortured rag –
an old cardigan perhaps, one black arm flung out –

The car glides clean above it. By good fortune and speed
rather than my careful manoeuvring,
no damage is done …
It's the sound of expiry in the seat beside me, the balloon-loss
of your breath

that sharpens my sight in hindsight –

brings me back from a dream of words
so that I see, too late, almost

                        yes, it *was* a tortoise,
a poured dark slick of animal life, following its risky neck
across the pelting highway.

Behind us are open-cut mines, pits of lead-grey waste,
chimneys which from a distance
look like the hooves
of giant mules, cast-off carapaces sweltering up
time turned toxic –

From our still point as we pass, we read the contradicting
signs, say *steam steam* and try to believe …

As now I try to believe it's still there, too – that chug in the
     mind
of muscles and flesh under an unpromising shell,
that wave in the void like a poem
sticking its neck out:

this tortoise, luminous in my rear-vision lake.

                                        Jean Kent

The Autobiography of Alice B. Toklas

You knew genius when you saw it, you said.
    Perhaps your cultivated
insignificance created shadow

    in which it shone more brightly. Gertrude Stein
was your own household genius, not so much loved
    as taken on, as an oriental monk

takes on the burden of the gods, whose service
    depends on order. Bells are rung
to rule, and certain kinds of sweeping must be done.

    For monks, it goes without saying
the gods are not indifferent to menu,
    or to trademarks, or to fashion

and all their foibles are a kind of glorious cheek.
    Because they can, they do
and this works well, as long as the god is stone.

But you are bolder and more knowing than monks
    and you want more. Because you know
that genius is not stone, because you understand

    how genius needs accomplices.
How like a blubbering child your genius is
    standing at the head of the stairs

uncombed, half-dressed and pleading for your kindness.
    You whisk by towards the kitchen.
Some third person is picking up its pen.

Joan Kerr

Song of the Beginning of the Night

The beginning of the night:
the deep ones have clear heads
in their shot glass cells
Truth lies to its family,
>   grabs its mother's dress, hurries
>   to a promise in the alley of madness

The beginning of night
>   The rose fires up again
>   while children remove their nicknames,
>   lovers their tails,
>   and love sweats gently
>   above a tender acacia

The beginning of night:
her beloved friends come out

>   to the edge of the heart
>   and burn wet stalks
>   pick a fight weaker than cotton,
>   and thoughts rub against the sesban plant

The beginning of night:
I emerge from my suspicions
and enter my neighbour's
I cry: who connected these memories to us,
and what is between us all – a cat slipping through the
    treacherous wall

The beginning of night:
jasmine slips a bribe into a policeman's nose,
asks:

do you have a heart, and a mother?
Blessings upon the mother that's given birth to two
children
and has filled out a little

Can you be other than who you are?

The beginning of night:
the houses answer, an ancient *salaam*.

Take a blanket
Take a pillow for your head

And blame unties your boot laces
And laughter clears your heart's lantern.
Peace be with you, and sand for your child to crawl upon.
When you come as a stranger,
Birds soon flutter in the branches

The beginning of night:
the sun stays up until morning

Ateif Khieri
(Translated by Timur Hammond)

Girl

The girl yearns to show you something
other than herself
though you will see only a girl, as long as
you possess nothing but your two eyes,
your parted mouth.

Listen
to the tribes take revenge from the water
beneath her eyebrows.
Armies of ants lend you sugar between two sips.
The warmth of parents cuts the neck and becomes a ring.
It pains the girl
when you set out,
when you desire something other than her.

Ateif Khieri
(Translated by Timur Hammond)

Reflectors: Drive 5

Part I

Admittedly I err by undertaking
This in its present form ...
—James Merrill

Sufficient time has passed to prompt
a test of memory. Sufficient time
to travel the road where weathers
and times of day are folded or blended
into one. Who drives? You and I or a family
member on the way to work or an appointment
in the city – notice how hard it is to focus
the journey towards luminescence,
always turning headlights back
towards an inner light. What properties
prefer an ownership, prefer a settlement
of coordinates and value? Back on the market,
the old place still has those horseshoes
turned upside down, embossed, water-marked
with luck running out, woven
through interlock mesh, glancing sideways
towards horse paddock and its vestigial
mushrooms, horses just light enough
to make something of gymkhana.
The twists and turns ignite.
As back through corners are past trees
in light burnished on spectrum's edge,
a pink-orange doused in greylight,
varieties of rust, tensions making stories
as shouts and demands to be let out
strand you always on a gravel corner,

at the thin end of a mega-burnout,
blacker than asphalt, zigzagging
over crests and sharp bends, a ledge,
devout dedication to annihilation –
the air thinner and evasive
where paddocks open out,
unreadable near mallee outcrops,
spiders pulling traps shut;
reflectors start to burn – chips
of speech, bytes of locution. By now
quarry owners would have undermined
the scarp, deceptively divided
road and habitat – admiring the view
no matter what it's built upon, admittedly
enjoying driving conditions where the road
expands. The car – a house, comfortable
in the lounge room, legs stretched out,
steering the television – remote control
sparking its redeye like a startled
but confident animal. But there's
no comparison, and the dead litter
roads everywhere there's scrub or trees or open space
where there's pollution not yet critical,
or critical and caught in a delayed reaction.
Who are we telling this? Who changes
radials when they're run down to snarling
hooks of metal? What details
can be added from here? The close-up
lost to panorama even where trees
attempt to close over, to cut out moonlight
or sick haloes of UFOs. We've seen them
up close – headlines that wouldn't rate
a line, like the thylacine seen at the eye
of the road, where the river is blood
in an optic nerve. I break, I swerve, I accelerate

into the curve. They seem not to want
to appreciate low ground, saltbush
and samphire, needles and Christmas spiders
that translate as tethered cities, aerial
cultures that don't come down until death:
insects caught on the mesh of the grille,
enfolded in the radiator: antifreeze and coolant,
maintaining 93 degrees centigrade as liquid
runs through the engine block, cylinder head,
the pump working as hard as a heart.
The pump as a heart? Vice versa?
Thermostat regulating flow?
Radiator: heat exchange, fins and tubes,
inlet and outlet, air flow, turbulator,
gnats, mosquitos, flies, and dozens, possibly
hundreds of species genetically compacted,
turbulated, distance on the clock increasing,
distance home decreasing
proportionally. Petition. Ask for
information. AKA. Lexical Englishes
here to deny trails and totems,
gathering on scrubby crests, around York gums,
crossing now-time journeys and non-time
transversals: 'Wandering' is a town further south
searching for displaced letters
and categories, a metathesis, a recall
of something read, elsewhere, or cogitated,
vacantly staring at particles run together,
like painstakingly compiled sequences
for a space-flick that takes a few seconds
of screen time ... days or weeks in the making.
Caught up on the side of the road: engine problems,
something entangles in the chassis,
a quick piss, searching back into darkness ...
reflectors inverting impact with a roo.

The motivation and cessation of bodily functions:
there's a high road-toll on this stretch ...
it's the weekender distances,
eye-soothing scenery, distance
between hotels and bottle shops.
Colloquial. Familiar. Dismissive –
it's dealt with like that, if not entirely forgotten,
prompted by small white crosses, a motorcycle helmet,
variable wreaths of non-cellulose flowers.
And a roo dragged into parrot bush: shreds of clothing
where the spiked leaves have hooked
a concerned passer-by. At high speed with the windows down
you can smell the bloated carcass. This is meat.
Occasion, survival, terror, trauma.
Seemed the dignified thing to do, what else ... Insurance
covered it, thank God. Shoved the grille
into the radiator, crushed fins,
impaired tubes ... those long-distance
dependencies, constrained by local
superstition, unbound by hopes of personal success –
of a faster car, or geographical distractions ...
a holiday in the mountains, or on an island so small
there are no straight lines, only corners.

John Kinsella

Happiness

After Robert Hass

Because on Sunday morning through the bedroom window
we saw six Rainbow Lorikeets
feasting on the blossom of the spindly fruit tree,
their brush-tipped tongues working down
into the open buds of the flowers, their red
and yellow breasts, their blue heads
suggesting the otherness of all creatures –

and because this morning
when I went into the study and lifted the blind,
I saw a pair of 'mostly gregarious' Bulbuls
on the branches right in front of me,
their black crests gelled into a punk cheekiness
suggesting the sameness of all creatures –

and because when I heard you coughing through the wall,
I remembered the other day at The Last Drop
when the coffees came with miniature teddy bear biscuits,
and you picked up your chocolate teddy with its one
missing leg and said, this is what
John Howard has done to our country
and we laughed, the six of us, glad
to be out and eating lunch.

One of the company, a writer, said
she couldn't write anything at the moment
because she was so happy,
despite the dreadful election result.
But happiness can push the pen as easily as misery.

You cough again and I recall how the scent
of your vanilla balm fills up the car,
I think of our daughter sitting on the fence
outside her classroom every Friday afternoon,
waiting for me to walk up, glance at my watch
and complain that they've rung the bell early again,
just so she can shake her head, grin
and scold me for being dependably, reliably, late.

Andy Kissane

Housing Estate
in the Howard Era

Modular mansions in pastels and creams,
'Entertainment areas' designed
around wide-screen TVs.
The windows are huge
but the curtains are drawn –
Pragmatism won't see it is ideology.

Fat-arsed cars are the local gods,
and double garages their shrines.
Gardens shrunk to lozenges and tabs,
and narrow paths to the washing lines.
More bedrooms than people.
These structures agree:
'Don't relate to the street.
Everything's inside, and for me.'

Mike Ladd

The Value of Peas

I am Eve Langley
and I know the value of peas.
They are sweeter than an Italian singer
on a winter morning.
They are Afghan kisses
that scatter like camel tracks
across the sand of my skin.
Eating one without thought will bankrupt you.
Their beauty – too perfect for a mouth to form words on,
and their tiny size holds the terror of the universe within it.

My babies, three sets of pea green eyes
who looked at me as if they knew me. What a mystery.
The Tasman's stopped hissing my name
And Gippsland's abandoned efforts to draw me back.

What was left behind by red-raw fingers
and cracked knees in the fertile dirt of my youth
where now nothing good can grow?

But I am not gone, I am here writing,
writing beneath that old crazy maker, the full moon,
that shivers and shines like a frost covered pea left too long
    on the vine.

Now I am where the towering trees and rocks
have pushed themselves up defiantly from the earth
to stake their claim before us.
There is no soft soil here for pathological rows of neatness
where nature's curves can be perfected to straighter tastes.
But I am not alone here in the Wildeness.
I have my peas,
and their company is more than I can bear.

Sandra E. Laight

Prayer

Oh, for my mother in her pain,
Almighty and all-loving Lord,
I come to plead with you again.

For years her body's been a bane
That's put all gladness to the sword:
Oh, for my mother in her pain!

Too much misery makes a stain
To black all light and block all laud:
I come to plead with you again.

Today at least relieve the strain
And give reprieve as a reward,
Oh, for my mother in her pain.

I know there is no other Name.
Despite the fact my faith is flawed,
I come to plead with you again.

Although my many sins maintain
That I deserved to be ignored –
Oh, for my mother in her pain
I come to plead with you again!

Andrew Lansdown

Stingers

In the scheme of stings,
bluebottles are less
than a minor irritation –
though who'd have guessed,
given their other name,
the one with cannon fire,
full blown sails, and a cross-
boned skull inside it.
At worst, on leaving the surf
in the wake of an encounter
with a Portuguese man-of-war,
your skin will be printed
with raised, red scribblings
such as some molluscs
and bloodworms make, at low tide,
and although the pain is akin
to having bad sunburn
raked repeatedly by fingernails,
relief is at hand: vinegar,
thistle milk, or a friend
who has the *fluido vitali*
in the lives of their palms.
But go further north, and swim
without a full body stocking
in the Arafura Sea, after
heavy rain, into the path
of a submarine bell
trailing live electrical wires,
and all remedies, tactile
and beyond the physical
will be laid to rest and waste.

A pulsing globe, with solar
panels and the lit filaments
of old amplifier valves
will oversee the donation
of your epidermis and the deeper
layers of your skin to science,
your central nervous system
to the ghost crabs and gulls.
Your lower back and thighs
will fast resemble a detail
from an aquatint etching
of someone flayed to ribbons
by a kelp whip, its sea-leather
strands infused with lashings
of coral snake venom,
and that's just the beginning.
If bluebottles play a minor role
in the linear, narrative film
that is the coastal education
for many Australian children,
and popping them with bare feet
at the high tide line
is both fun and retribution –
then box jellyfish, sea wasps,
or whatever you'd care to call
these projections of fear
and fascination with our
offshore, killer nature –
they will always remain,
for those who made it clear
of the water, as reminders
of how the word 'agony' falls
so far short of the mark
as to render it redundant.

It's easy, from the sand,
to say how waves are made
all the more beautiful
by having flotillas
of blue, current-dependent
pockets of air, and the more
heavily armed wanderers
we know, collectively,
as stingers moving around
inside them – but consider
the man who was stung
while stroking out off a beach at Cairns:
    Waiting to die, he saw
harbour lights coming on
in the shallows, and because
hearing is the last
of the senses to go, he heard,
from somewhere close
or distant, like an invitation
to a funeral or a healing,
a water bird ask *Are you with me?*
and then, from somewhere else,
as if accepting, on his behalf,
the invitation to a healing,
another water bird answered
Yes, yes, yes.

                         Anthony Lawrence

live crab a la cordon bleu a la S

cradled in the silk of the summer sun
the crab reflects on language
on S dominating his world;
on salt, sea, sand and sky, on summer
sun sex and search, on survival and self,

never contemplating a live show of steam
chorus of simmer salt stir sip, stir
on scream, silent still on stunned;

on once in the silk of the summer sun.

Josef Lesser

Luminous Alias

The strangeness will wear off
—Jackson Pollock

You passed out, you don't understand.
Those years were stolen from me.
I think I made friends with the slobs of Hollywood and
    perished up there.
I travel light, but this is too light.

I *was* conscious, like a child bride.
I lived in their villas, ricocheted through the halls of fame,
radiating love, going for the jugular.
Wound up further away than anyone.

I was down in Hell discussing redemption.
All my dreams came true so fast.
Long primrose nights are coming back to haunt me,
nearly the only pleasure left.

I'm sorry if I added darkness,
but I couldn't just show up empty-handed.
Time to cut and run, sort of a polka.
Even the rain is black. Is everybody helpless here?

Keep your eyes on the road, that's a kind of kissing.
We're bound for nowhere, it's a beautiful place —
somewhere between serenity and vertigo.
I'm grown up. Please allow me to show you.

It's peaceful here. Any comment?
I know that's my life flashing up there on the screen.
I travel light, but this is too light.
Enough of the games. Tell me what I already know.

Emma Lew

The General

Her life's a battlefield
bodies lie around her but she's erect
giving commands to the grass and trees.

The officers died first and other generals next.
Now a few locals and other ranks –
who she overlooked, appear
from time to time on the horizon
where dusk is staining the clouds.
Sometimes they bring her sustenance
but it's dangerous work
she's still got ammunition
and her gun's well greased
with ire and discipline.

Nobody's happy,
the local's don't like it –
they must bury the dead.
Bereft and amazed she stands
her ground courageously
counting her bullets
seething with plans.

Kate Llewellyn

The Wedding

1.
There'd been no honey, no moon,
the actor's star blazing in mid-shoot
of a Pagewood film. Straight from the Registry
to the Long Bar, then Florentino's for dinner
and into a cab, back to the flat

at the Cross. Two floors up in a racketty lift.
Rooms he'd shared with his first wife
the luscious Crystal and his mother, greenly ageing.
Until Crystal had left him. For someone else.
And then his mother. For eternity.

2.
Lilla's wedding night for four – Crystal's
douche-can still looped from its hook
behind the bathroom door; her showgirl
photo albums stacked, leaning like Pisa.
In the kitchen, dinted saucepans, a gas-singed

cosy. The grey terrazzo sink, where the mother last
clutched his hand to the seismic shift of her heart.
(The ménage à trois.) (Lilla cannot imagine!)
That's just the way it was is all he'll allow.
As though Lilla might be some passing tourist
who can't read 'Keep Off the Grass'.

3.
Lilla unpacks her trousseau. Pearl-lustre,
full-length satin to cling. Her hips, her behind,
the vulnerable small of her back.
In the mirror (smoothing the flow
of her body) halted by the indent of elastic
around her waist, she watches herself lift
the nightdress and slowly shockingly
slip the panties down. In its fall the satin
crackles, burns.
      Night-night, he says. Then
a cheek kiss. And the blank screen of his back.

                     Yve Louis

Foxfall I

Stiv Pret, Master Spy
—Belgrade TV

No one ever spies a lot, perhaps.
If you think of Kim Philby, you remember
his pet fox, Jackie, slipped or thrown
from his roof, that gorgeous phrase:
'Full Colonel in the KGB', not really
whatever it was he told them, although
in fact he told them names, and
people died. He still spied, obsessive,
apparently, while he wrote for the *Observer*,
in a mode which was left-wing, but
not excessive. In fact, his belief –
or rather, his heartless passion –
grew much clearer in private obsession,
                              like a fever,
and none of that remotely fits this case.
                    Confusion:
when one observes for Nato, one is simply
observing for Nato, although the subject
opposed Nato bombing and still would, as
counter-productive, but information
is charity's petrol and leaks
everywhere from its engine, as if blood.
We deal also with confession. The tongue
is a soft spy-master.

Confession, conversation and conversion
are charity's currency, current, all good
for energising a depressed ex-major,
politician, schoolgirl, or princess, as
if blood. After being a warrior, charity
is the next best thing, because privacy
is not one of its problems. Torture could
be often one of its problems, however,
                              and even if one tried
one can't resign from charity, for all
that leaves one is confession, as if bled: no
poison on the street, no
matter what was said: no
foxfall on the street, too quick for blood.

Jennifer Maiden

Foxfall 2
An Aura of Evening

Ascending to anonymity, an 'Australian-born
US diplomat' is quoted on the Sydney news
as saying the Israeli bombing of Lebanon
is not Israel's fault, but that
        of Hezbollah. His face
shines linear grey, an aura of evening
and business, but on the news
he is not given a name, rather
as if this gave his pronouncements
an authority identity might lose.
        Beirut
loses another power station, but it
is used to burning, shock
is absent from the equation. On
both sides of the border, apprehension
has a strange sugar taste
from exhaustion. Perhaps it is an odder
fate to surf the sugars of ambition,
one's sense-of-self in flame, like some
bombed source of electricity, upon
the evening news as nameless as an orphan.

Jennifer Maiden

Foxfall 3
Significance

I die happy, but I pity you. It don't signify,
my dearest, dearest Liz.
—last words of Charles James Fox, Regency leader
and founder of His Majesty's Opposition

It's the first thing one thinks when drunk
and one hopes also the last
thing one thinks when dying: things
don't signify in desperate sequence
as one always felt or feared. Foxes
in Asian mythology disguise
themselves as lovely women, to lure
travellers to disaster. Sometimes
one mistakes a ghost for a fox, but
ghosts are supposedly better. Lately
the local foxes along the Nepean
have looked skinny and bedraggled,
glancing over their shoulders at the car
with headlight eyes. They don't like
the Lakes Scheme either: the machinery,
the mosquitos, the weeds and the constant water.
Rowers are not like foxes, replace
slink with sequence. Charles James
Fox is one of my heroes. When I taught
uni classes, I read them his speech
against the Napoleonic Wars, when Pitt
had decided on a pause to test Napoloeon:
That man, sir, is not writhing
in agony, he is pausing. That one
is not dead, he only pauses. Oh, yes,

I remember without quoting. There
never was such rhetoric, such
proper propaganda, and all of it
made into an institution, under
the patronage of a prince. Charles James
Fox was a great gambler, fearless
always about the win, the losses, a lover
to such a degree of defiance that
he married his Liz in secret, in terror
he'd be thought not living in sin. He seems,
a lover of the masses,
to have been greasy and dark and adored
especially on the hustings, but his speeches
build sequence and repetition like
a confident, cunning, passionate palace.
On a lonely road, you meet a fox
and find it a lovely woman. You
apologise for the Lakes Scheme, the
weather, the poison, the whole
bushy new millennium, its malice,
its killer smile and phantom techno-shares.
She is gracious, her layered clothes
are cumulative like a palace, she
is dark, untidy, slippery
and jewelled by March rain, her eyes
big and dead as artificial lakes.
She says she only paused, like you,
            alone
between one point and another: 'Apparently,
enough words will make a system to
outlast a millennium, although
I repeat it doesn't signify, and there
never was a thing you could have done.'

Jennifer Maiden

'Together We Will
a Cheese Achieve'

—*George W. Bush on the situation in
the Korean Peninsula*

Also: 'It will take a long time to achieve
chaos', on Iraq. This, a journo who
actually worked for Rupert, thought
frankly 'terrifying'. But do the 'heh heh
heh's with which Junior punctuates
his little errors indicate
perhaps something cosier, more meant:
lethal little injections which
gauge decadence's deep greed for
the simple?   The syntax of Gump
wins through.   The blossomy white
bush behind Bush in the cheese speech
has subliminal softness, the not-quite
monkey face has innocence, begs
to be saved from the lab at last.
Defending scarring with hot
wire his college's initiates, Frat
President W. declared that one 'used
branding irons in Texas.'

If the French were 'cheese-eating
surrender monkeys', what cheese
will be achieved to feed us?
If George's functional dyslectic
has metaphor's grace, what cheese
is this he makes? It is a new synthesis:
                a brie with a crust
like golden toast, clear water oozing
out from under like a gunshot
wound: a camembert like cake; old
cheddar like warm wormwood: something
very smelly, very sweet, kept safe
by its scars of simple mould.

Jennifer Maiden

Midnight Drive

Tonight I'm climbing
the freeway's hot darkness

past the white bull shoulders
of the semis

the hill slopes holding moonlight
the starboard of the road

scarred with white lamps
that are not lamps

only reflections
I cannot pass.

I wish you pain, silently
like a prayer

for bringing me here

an hour's drive
and every second
further from home.

Annette Marner

Songs for Paul

'Beware the fury of a patient man'
                    John Dryden

1.
Handsome as Adam in your car mirror,
leaves from the clearing still stuck
to the back of your jacket.

2.
That got your nose open, didn't it?
Her scratches on you. The sweet
rank pussy smell on you as you swagger
into the café, looking around, head held high.

3.
You dream of nipples, music. What is it she likes,
Mozart, Beethoven? Something like that.

4.
The highway. All those radio tunes written
too late to help you. Illinois, Virginia,
the Carolinas. That skinny blonde
who stole your wallet afterwards.

5.
Late May.
Guess she's had the kid by now.
Little bastard.

6.
Whiskey helps. Another bottle helps even more.

7.
Onscreen at the drive-in there's always some girl
who falls and twists her ankle. She'll be scared, pausing
on unlit stairs as your new date wipes her mouth and
zips you up. The car reeks of popcorn, beer, semen.

8.
You dream of an empty theatre, you alone in the seats
waiting for you to come onstage.

9.
The boys at the factory will love it. You can tell them
you were at it all night, and how she wept when you left.

10.
One day you will stare into yet another cheap motel mirror
at the face of an out-of-breath, fat stranger.

11.
She never did come back.

12.
It is already too late for the magic you once laughed at.

13.
No cheating now. Spell rescue. Don't look.
Spell ruin. Spell empty well. Spell memory.

Ian McBryde

Entropy

I see life as a roadside inn where I have to
stay until the coach from the abyss pulls up.
—Fernando Pessoa

You said to walk without
caring to walk, attend concerts
without hearing the music, to
use forceps to take yourself
from yourself:

Such energy you put into this Tao
of nothing, distaste for others
that lacks all arrogance, the
individual soul a witless bird
flitting here, flitting there.

Life an accumulation of dreary
Sunday afternoons. The well
and the sky staring at each other
with no chance of seeing.

Your bottle of wine is left
half full, half empty. The coach
that might take you from nowhere
to nowhere is unaccountably
held up, delayed, but not
indefinitely.

You have no choice but to wait.

Shane McCauley

Anger

Hysterical animal banging
    in the box of night that
    your brain becomes.

Harm migrates across
    the swampy distances
    of your mouth.

Your body, merely grass
    distorted by the wind
    raking over a hill.

There is a script for
    such chaos, though it
    can never be remembered,

this occult confusion
    that disguises
    itself as clarity.

David McCooey

Jubilate Agony

After Christopher Smart

For I will consider my Prime Minister, Johnny.

For he sits curled at the far right hand of God, and knows what the left is doing.

For he is the cat that has got the cream and his Cheshire grin will not disappear.

For we have invoked him thrice and his spoor can be found now in every house.

For having received votes and won office he begins to consider the media.

For them he performs in ten degrees.

For first he looks upon his perpetually clean conscience.

For secondly he grooms himself assiduously.

For thirdly he attunes his antennae whiskers, that he may know his adversaries.

For fourthly he pricks up his ears, that he may hear what they say about him.

For fifthly he extends his retractable claws.

For sixthly are his claws sharpened by minions.

For seventhly are his minions sharpened by claws.

For eighthly he sprays his scent where he will, to establish there is no limit to his ministry.

For ninthly on his hind paws he prances, his little pink penis waving like a flag.

For tenthly he purrs his soporific purr until all good kittens are sleeping.

For having considered the media and himself he will consider his enemies.

For when he takes his prey he is merciless.

For one mouse in seven escapes to the backbench.

For he counteracts the powers of Labor by his electoral sins and glaring lies.

For he counteracts Beazley, who is fat, by brisking about the block.

For in his morning walks he loves the media and the media love him.

For he is of the tribe of President.

For the Cat Prime Minister is a term of the Tiger President.

For he has the hissing of a serpent which in public he suppresses.

For he will do destruction and be well fed, and he will spit when he is cornered.

For he purrs in thankfulness when George tells him he's a good cat.

For he is a blunt instrument for public schoolchildren in their learning.

For every university is incomplete under him, a spirit lacking in his blessing.

For he is a fan of Andrew Lloyd Webber, but not of T.S. Eliot.

For he will not say sorry to Mr. Mistoffelees, the Original Conjuring Cat.

For he has surpassed even Macavity, who was called the Hidden Paw.

For he now can not only defy, but can create the Law.

For his supporters suffer from the Stockholm Syndrome.

For they do not have to stand in queues, which is patience upon approbation.

For they do not have to fetch and carry, which is patience in unemployment.

For they do not have to jump over sticks, which is proof positive for Centrelink.

For the ease of his defense is an instance of the love of the media to him exceedingly.

For he knows that the media is his saviour.

For he is a master of camouflage.

For he is the most pernicious of tomcats.

For he is of the Lord's rich, and so indeed is he called by the rich perpetually – Help Johnny! Help Johnny! The poor are biting at our throats.

For I curse the name of *his* Lord Jesus that the rich are made richer.

For his tongue is like sandpaper and he has whittled us to the bone.

For he is loved by the hypocrite and the miser.

For the former has no fear of detection.

For the latter escapes the charge.

For he backs the camel through the eye of the needle at the first notion of big business.

For he made a great figure in Afghanistan and Iraq for his signal services.

For he has captured his Icneumon rat, and detained it indefinitely.

For his motions upon the face of the country are more destructive than any other quadraped.

For his voters have blessed him and the variety of his crimes.

For he can tread to all the measures upon a march.

For I am a poor cat and must swim for my life.

For claws don't kill people, cats do.

For he is a creep.

Mal McKimmie

Some Things the Body Knows

1.

The sight of a tiger snake at the end of winter
brings you into its world
where softness never evolved
and to live is to be thin and armoured
in the dinosaur stripes of the grass.
In the world of snakes to wake is urgency,
every movement desperate as an action-hero's.
For half a year the amphetamine sun pours out of the sky,
then half a year of recovery dreaming like stones.

2.

Carved stones, bronzes, shards move slowly towards you
out of antiquity, disrupting the nervous system
with their quiet radiation. They shift
the world too, but stay within the human,
changing things subtly like deletion of a few words from a
     language.
A night disturbed by Pictish symbol stones,
watching comb and mirror change to bird change to beast
makes history literally a nightmare from which you're trying
     to wake.
Or closer to home the women's asylum with its crossed out
     windows
still stops thoughts in their tracks sudden as shock-treatment.

Graeme Miles

Street Preacher
– Surfers Paradise

His mouth is a wild dog.
If you listen carefully
there is a mating call
wandering along Main Beach,
crying out that his body is in pain,
that he needs to create a palace
inside himself

It doesn't make sense
that he will walk down Cavill Avenue
singing hymns to the tourists,
that he will turn over pages of the sea
to search for a secret dog –
that he will howl at the sky
until the moon turns black –
and a pale bitch
invites him into the fog
behind her eyelids

John Millett

Widows at Jupiters Casino

They bleed into the night
and head for Jupiters Casino.
Its lights will rescue each one
from a secret catheter
buried in the wall of an IT ward.

They are caged birds and ring
ghost bells in the Fruit Machines –
golden girls once,
they burn with memories
of dead lovers, buried
in sad graveyards with no windows.

When they arrive at Jupiters
neon lights comb their hair.
A plastic surgeon has shaped
their smiles. Money has perfumed
the cars bellboys park.
Their bank accounts are full
of bruises and old wounds,
full of fangs that gnawed
at the world's poor until
death was a high tide mark.

I watch them wade through
the darkness. They are so fragile
even the night air
dares not touch them.

John Millett

Voyager

It could start here again,
summer on the edge of instant war

night flowering under courage
stole from municipal stars

where olive leaves
in freshly graded parks

look slight lossy in the breeze,
definition soft

& dry as moonlight.
The cities will all fall

into an open sky,
your epidermis tracked by satellites

will barely strike a shadow
in the fusive afterglow

of hydrocarbon jets.
So goodbye, go out & find

what there is to say
of transformation, the sparkle, junk

& greenest hearts. Go out
before the world knows you're not.

Peter Minter

Post-Orientalism

Baudelaire never made it to India,
sent there in '41 by his mother and stepfather
to cure his dissolute ways, his flânerie,
his ratbaggery and incurable genius.

Couldn't they see that a trip *là-bas* could only feed the fever?
So of course he agreed, embarking on a steamer at Le Havre,
with enough opium and books to keep him company;
the ship's chambermaid also, mesmerised no doubt
by his melancholy and his outlandish style.

The captain spoke of his percentage in the Compagnie des
    Indes,
and the propagation of vanilla in Réunion and Madagascar
while prising the wine carafe gently from young Charles' grip.

At Saint-Denis he descended, under instructions,
the sea so rough that landing from the launch required
    climbing a rope ladder
hanging at the end of a jetty, two cannon balls attached to
    the bottom end.
'Grab the rungs at the crest of the wave, no sooner,' they
    yelled.
But Baudelaire, the formalist, the agent of urbanity, insisted on
climbing the ladder with books under his arm,
and slowly, pursued by the next rising wave,
reaching and engulfing him and tearing him from the ladder.
Then fished out (with some difficulty) but, amazingly, the
    books unrelinquished.
So finally he consented (*Voyons, Monsieur! Enfin!*) to leave
    them in the boat.

And on his way up again, rinsed gently by another wave.
Kept hold, arrived on top and set off for the town, calm and
    cool,
his hat turning and drifting in the Indian Ocean depths.

The immersion transforms the oeuvre, or is it
Emmelina de Bragard, a creole woman *aux charmes ignorés*
whom he knew
    in a perfumed country caressed by the sun
    under a canopy of trees ablaze with purple.

Baudelaire, our urban dandy, is suddenly provincialised.
Standing wet and dripping on a jetty in the Indian Ocean,
the aesthetic hemispheres turn: now he will invent
from *là-bas*
    a modernism metropolises never knew.
Oceanic feeling now flows, unstoppable, from the 'exploited'
    places
(whose spices and perfumes literally funded the literatures of
    the modern,
giving the bourgeoisie time, money, dissolution).

The war of economic domination is won as soon as declared.
But now the postcolonial subjects set up shop
in the tourist-infected tropics, with an inexhaustible resource:
the forever incomplete desires for *luxe*, *calme* and *volupté*.
And sure, they spin a subtle, but substantial, economic revenge.

Like a strange and beautiful Trojan horse, our Indian Ocean
    poet
released an army of weird desires into the metropolis:
such an infection is never, ever misrepresentation.
You cannot argue with a virus or a verse, it takes hold, or not.

Stephen Muecke

The Nostril Songs

P. Ovidius Naso
when banished from Rome
remained in the city
for days on slave clothing,
for weeks in his study,
for decades in living noses –

★

Trees register the dog

and the dog receives the forest
as it trots toward the trees

then the sleeping tiger
reaches the dog en masse
before the dog reaches the tiger:

this from the Bengal forests
in the upper Kerosene age,

curry finger-lines in shock fur.

★

The woman in the scarlet tapestry
who stands up on a sprigged cushion
of land in space, is in fact
nude, as all are in the nostril-world.

What seem to be her rich gowns
are quotations from plants and animals
modulating her tucked, demure
but central olfactory heart

and her absent lover, pivoting
on his smaller salt heart
floats banner-like above her.

★

No stench is infra dog.

★

Fragrance stays measured,
stench bloats out of proportion:
even a rat-sized death,
not in contact with soil, is soon
a house-evacuating metal gas
in our sinuses; it boggles our gorge.
No saving that sofa:
give it a Viking funeral!

★

The kingdom of ghosts
has two nostril doors
like the McDonald's symbol.

You are summoned to breathe
the air of another time
that is home, that is desperate,
the tinctures, the sachets.

You yourself are a ghost.
If you were there
you are still there –

even if you're alive
out in the world of joking.

For other species, the nasal kingdom
is as enslaved and barbed
as the urine stars around all territory,

as the coke lines of autumn
snorting into a truffle-pig's head

or the nose-gaffed stallion,
still an earner, who screams rising
for the tenth time in a day.

★

Mammal self-portraits
are everywhere, rubbed on
or sprayed on in an instant.

Read by nose, they don't give
the outline shapes demanded
by that wingless bird the human;

with our beak and eyes
we perceive them as smears
or turds, or nothing at all.

Painted from inside
these portraits give the inner
truth of their subject

with no reserve or lie.
Warned or comforted or stirred
every mammal's an unfoolable

connoisseur, with its fluids
primed to judge, as it moves
trapped in an endless exhibition.

★

Half the reason for streets,
they're to walk in the buzz
the sexes find vim in,
pheromones for the septa
of men and of women.

★

If my daddy isn't gone
and I smell his strength and care
I won't grow my secret hair
till a few years later on
on Tasmania. Down there.

★

When I was pregnant
says your sister, my nose
suddenly went acute:
I smelled which jars and cartons
were opened, rooms away,
which neighbours were in oestrus,
the approach of death in sweat.
I smelt termites in house-framing
all through a town, that mealy taint.
It all became as terrible
as completely true gossip
would be. Then it faded,
as if my baby had learned
enough, and stopped its
strange unhuman education.

★

A teaspoon upside down
in your mouth, and chopping onions
will bring no tears to your cheeks.
The spoon need not be silver.

★

Draw the cork from the stoic age
and the nose is beer and whisky.
I'll drink wine and call myself sensitive!
was a jeer. And it could be risky.

Wesleyans boiled wine for Communion;
a necked paper bag was a tramp;
one glass of sweet sherry at Christmas,
one flagon for the fringe-dwellers' camp.

You rise to wine or you sink to it
was always its Anglo bouquet.

★

When we marched against the government
it would use its dispersant gas
Skunk Hour. Wretched, lingering experience.
When we marched on the neo-feudal
top firms, they sprayed an addictive
fine powder of a thousand hip names
that was bliss in your nostrils, in your head.
Just getting more erased our other causes
and it was kept illegal, to be dear,
and you could destroy yourself to buy it
or beg with your hands through the mesh,
self-selecting, as their chemists did say.

★

Mars having come nearest our planet
the spacecraft Beagle Two went
to probe and sniff and scan it
for life's irrefutable scent,
the gas older than bowels: methane,
strong marker of digestion from the start,
life-soup-thane, amoeba-thane, tree-thane.
Sensors would screen Ares' bouquet
for paleo- or present micro-fartlets,
even one-in-a-trillion pico-partlets,
so advanced is the state of the art.
As Mars lit his match in high darkness
Beagle Two was jetting his way.

★

In the lanes of Hautgout
where foetor is rank
Gog smites and Pong strikes
black septums of iron
to keep the low down.
Ride through, nuzzle your pomander:
Don't bathe, I am come to Town:

Far ahead, soaps are rising,
bubble baths and midday soaps.
Death to Phew, taps for Hoh!
Cribs from your Cologne water.

★

Ylang ylang
elan élan
the nostril caves
that breathe stars in
and charm to Spring
the air du temps
tune wombs to sync
turn brut men on
Sir Right, so wrong −
scent, women's sense
its hunters gone
not its influence!
nose does not close
adieu sagesse

Les Murray

They

soon will arrive, knock, on the bluestone slab
utter dropping – signs of excitement
thumping, groping, hidden
blackbirds in mating seasons
stained cranes that had burned into atomic
the whole lot in the fey rain
in the ash, fake
years, eleven exactly, there I was conceived
Saturn had done the gorging, Medea the sub
zeroing in, the falling
of whole house, Kabuki eruptions, knowledge,
namings, christenings, rites of wronging
the other, dedications, mementos as if
nothing had really

Nguyen Tien Hoang

Horizon

is gentle geometry, the Tao of Euclid.
Not quite time or place, it boasts no deity,
is democratic but elusive, we never see our own.
What of tomorrow and all your line?
The margin moves as they sail in –
the least mast tip's all you'll discern
for it's round as second chance
yet holds none.
Even dreams embrace no final rim,
waking is just meniscus,
though the stranger's smile, returned,
is a shared border, a lifting of tariffs.
Some wear their threshold like a cloak
or suck it dry.
Some turn theory edge-on
and push their people over:
Argentina's beaten silver,
Rwanda, Srebrenica, ploughed under,
Cambodia's stacked-up grins.

Jan Owen

From *beached rd*

nothing happening
but a series of minor events
trivia on the loose

the blonde
her legs like whips in jeans
back towards me
and kicking junk into the gutter
of her lawn
before her house yanks her back inside

that anaemic alsatian
nosing around the fresh grass
for something intangible

a kid racing his bike along the pavement
and tugging a string held one-handed
while trying to scoop air into a plastic bag
and mostly failing

another complaining
that he can't stop the water
as a trickle trickles along the gutter
and through his fingers

shoppers trying to force themselves
to buy a packet or can of something or other
to keep them interested

the gums soggy and without their galahs
because the air is humourless
and barely bearing to carry themselves

outersuburbia seeming forever
no terror that time has stopped
bleached of emotion

that every decent-sized event has been cut up
into a series
of minor casualties

grazed knees on gravel and asphalt

can you hear me, mate? i want you to come out without the firearm.
i want you to come out now. to work it out

    the aluminium body cruises king william st.
    blank skins stripped off faces
    blurt out words that fall
    to asphalt/
                          splintered tinsel
    lips/& hands/dentures/toes/erections
hair/periods/of pain
        tow & rattle along behind the bus
        like cans tied to a honeymoon car
a head falls off/rocks & rolls towards its destination/
           a cock/a cunt

    the town hall rises into the night
    a clock churns away on the cock/3 sides
    for voyeur participation/black hands
        that wipe over a white face
        & keep time straight
                if time stops
                the tower subsides
                & the govt. falls

        every major city in australia has one

a punk dances at a party
with a rifle slung over his back
& dressed in khaki fatigues

a woman seems impressed with the uncertainty of the
                                        intention
it seems a good line   the violent question-mark
                              which dribbles from her mouth
                            some woman dances with a queen
                            he zips her up
                            she flashes thick red lips
                            a red dress
                            plenty of pink gum

i don't believe in objectivity
i do believe in everything being visual

                    & if you believe in exploitation
                    first show me the victim/
                                    or non-victim

i can't find a morality of good & bad
in this closet of make-believe
                    only power exists
                            & your ability to make everyone
                            believe you're right/
                            your way is the successful way
                            to survival

some people eat heads
some people eat testicles
some don't eat at all
the winner survives to burn your theories
to ignore them or accept them
                        at a whim

a humiliation is being the subject
of someone else's whim/chains on the hands
                              & mouth

all these faces eating spiced chicken leg
licking their lips over
& you can't tell who's a homosexual/bisexual/heterosexual
                you can't live by voice alone

the toilet as a place to meet graffiti
shake hands with yourself
& clothes/
                clothes are only an indicator
                sometimes
                                skin & hands
                                across a sea of urine

masturbating up the arse

Neil Paech

From *Freehold*

1.
Dear Mother, I am here at last
under canvas on the Clarence –
two good shepherds to assist
Thomas Ryan and Cedric Parslow –
and fifteen hundred head of sheep
we brought up from the Hunter.

The property's for leasing only,
fifteen thousand acres,
but soon I mean to have it freehold,
the river frontage to begin with.
Kooringal is the name I'll keep
following the natives
who say that that's the term they use
a half day up and down the river.

I've had some good acquaintance with
the Bundjalung from when I worked
with Ogilvie at Yulgilbar
those two short years ago.
I have my first few dozen words
and something of the grammar.
Their attitude is friendly here
despite some problems at Ramornie,
a station nearer town.
There was some blood at Yulgilbar
which never is much mentioned.
After which my friend up there
managed his agreement with them
back in '42.
It seems also to cover me

a little further down.
I'm hoping I can hire a few
of these fine Bundjalung young men
to help me with the fencing.
Tobacco, flour and blankets maybe –
or maybe some small wage.
Ryan and Parslow aren't so sure
but they should soon agree.
I'm hopeful that relations here
between us white and black
will be as good as Yulgilbar's –
or even rather better.
I think we'll rub along quite well.

You will have read of 'massacres'
and 'native depredations'
scattered through the London press
but that's a phase I think has passed
in this part of the country.

I've met a handful of my neighbours
from when I was with Ogilvie
and do suspect my attitudes
will not be widely shared.
Charles Tindall, downstream at Ramornie,
is certainly one such.
That episode at the Orara
is much remembered there, it seems.
The Whitbys, too, across the river,
a family I've yet to meet,
are of the same persuasion.

Some months must pass before you read this
snug beside your fire in Kent –
and think of me beside the Clarence,

sitting up by candle-light,
penning in my first-night tent.

Soon, I do assure you, mother,
there'll be a fine slab hut —
and, after that, a homestead too
will surely grace Kooringal.
It may not match the Ogilvies'
ambition for a German *Schloss*
but it will do us Coaldales credit,
have no doubt on that.

It may be days before I have
the chance to send this off by horse
towards 'The Settlement'
(yet to gain its name, I fear).

I thought, dear mother, I should write
some record of my first day here,
and this, my first night on Kooringal.

Your loving youngest, Edward.

2.
Dearest Amy, I've just heard
of something that must interest you —
a new arrival on the river,
a bachelor of twenty-eight
with fifteen thousand acres.
'Surely that is not so huge,'
I seem to hear you say.
But he is young and well-connected,
fine family back in Kent,
father in the Navy somewhere,
all that kind of thing.

The rumour is he speaks quite well –
and likes to wear a dinner suit
if manners should require it.

Edward Coaldale is his name.
I know that much at least.
a protégé of Ogilvie's,
who first came up two years ago
to help at Yulgilbar –
and then went back to get his sheep
and finalise the lease.
No freehold yet apparently
except the homestead block.
He has some carpenters already
running up his house –
or so I hear from Sarah Whitby
there across the river.

You do know Sarah Whitby, don't you,
youngest of the Whitby clan?
Came out at the Race Club Ball.
She says he's quite good-looking in
a sunburned sort of way.
Quite a worker, too, they say.

The only problem so far is
his attitude to blacks.
Likes to use the local types
as shepherds when required.
Apparently he's learned the lingo
or quite a deal of it.

There's been no cattle-spearing yet
but he's been known, our Sarah says,
to offer them a 'killer'.

Her father William is, she says,
always 'very firm' with blacks.
He just won't let them on his land –
and that, he says, is that.

Young Coaldale thinks quite differently.
But this will prove a fad, I trust,
and quite soon fade away.

It takes a while to understand
the way things work along the Clarence.
Edward Coaldale will, I'm sure,
turn out to be an asset.
The men in this whole valley tend
to be a disappointing lot.
Stock diseases, market prices ...
they have no conversation really.
Our Mr Coaldale should be welcome.

But don't you be forgetting, Amy,
I'm the one who saw him first,
I, your good friend, Cindy Tindall,
signing off for now.

Geoff Page

His Literary Reputation

Already posthumous, I know I am ignored.
Unlike pulp fiction I am pulped
or found, perhaps, in a remainder shop.
A poet is a figure nailed to wood,
a public sculpture held in private storage.

There was one who parodied my early
style exquisitely; the best of those he did.
When he collected all he'd written,
he edited my echo from his book.
He anticipated I would waste away.

I gave pleasure to about a dozen,
none of whom was an opinion maker.
Anthologists have never bothered.
The skill-less, boring, unrhythmical and glib
occupy the Golan Heights of fashion.

Now I have sweet privilege of hindsight
before events, I know I make mistakes.
I think the power of lyric is its clearness;
explanation is the opposite of worth.
Reincarnated, I would be obscure.

K.F. Pearson

Leafing Through the Latin Dictionary

fuga, fugas – music now, not back
at school where Harry Roberts flashed his gown,
a toga to berate a class as slack
as Rome became; we'd been meant to be
English Augustans, but were soon brought down
to being worthy only of a few
emotive Saxon nouns and verbs: the sea
had brought our Fathers to a sanded shore,
packed tight with iron sermons on The Poor –
but still the dictionary had work to do:
peregrinus, wanderers in need
of some Virgilian outcome – might this book
have shown how Europe's words could safely bleed
on strands Aeneas left to Captain Cook?

oppidanus – not from Rome, but not
from Eton either: if from anywhere
we hailed from pissed-on concrete and caked snot,
a gravel-rash battalion called up for
training in Real Estate and Prostate snips –
no worse for that, but somewhere off there lurked
a world whose words were from a greater law,
the Pax Britannica, a king in sight,
an Empire wider than a day and night,
the home boys set to die among the ships –
spero, spes – we hoped and now it's here,
the Trading-up Republic, confident
of its own sparky Roman atmosphere
and *timeo*, to fear the gifts we're sent.

Peter Porter

By Whose Permission
Do These Angels Serve?

Though there are laws of Physics and Thermodynamics
there are no enforcers or permit granters. Most of us
don't see the angels, or perhaps what we do not see
is angelic polystyrene, ectoplasm purposefully set
to hold the world in place. This is what transforms
Nature to Theology; there is no logic, no connection
other than angelic holding-hands. How otherwise
could the lawful and unfinished cruelty of existence
ring us on a sapphire day with its insistence
on life's invincibility, our being here the product
of evolution's terror-tang? If X is humorous,
can he be also moving? If emotionally profound,
will Y still be inventive? And now Z calls on some
prosthetic angel to move in mordent dreams
to close his grave up; he sees in strangers' faces
the fellow-candour of a trap. Angels should not be named –
beside a sea, at castle top, in poems by named poets –
they are the air which helps invisibility
to thicken, and have to serve so no angelic waste
might threaten Heaven. Easy to imagine angels
as flamingos wading in a lake, and quite like God,
being neighbourly and pink each day at dawn.

Peter Porter

There is a River

i.m. Janet

The newly dead slip over you like a shirt,
black, silken, rustling as beetles
and the shirt becomes invisible
or, wearing it, you become yourself invisible.
You'll have no conversation with the newly
dead. Their bodies of such pain
hunger for blankness, for the nothing
of crushed wet flowers.
There is a river and a girl swimming
farther away, beyond all you remember.

Craig Powell

Sugarloaf Sequence

1. Bypassing vertigo

Bypassing vertigo
you down
   down
a shandy of sky
        water
           silence,
from high on the top of the dam wall
that leans against the Sugarloaf

draining almost to your bared self
for all the sweetness
until you pull up
   wincing

on a nerve of raw clay
   exposed with thoughtless emptying.

You measure its widening
against the high water mark
stained by a far-off admirer
on the base of your memory.

      But what must be done?

Your tongue rolls
   clear
way clear
   of the question
as you suck carefully on
cool   cool heaven.

2. *Antiphonal Notes*

After A Steady Storm of Correspondence: Selected letters
of Gwen Harwood 1943-1995, *edited by Gregory Kratzmann*

Bell-birds pluck antiphonal notes
on the banks of the Sugarloaf cool and green,
summoning a dream spell halcyon and remote.

You think of a friend's letters often closed
with *mit ewiger liebe**. Unseen
bell-birds pluck antiphonal notes.

Above the canopy the high sounds float
non-stop, keeping both closeness and space between,
summoning a dream spell halcyon and remote,

of children you've known who have no doubt,
who'd run hand in hand through the trees
where bell-birds pluck antiphonal notes

out into the stillness of the open slopes;
who'd zigzag like wallaby around shadows they see
summoning a dream spell, halcyon and remote.

No distance, no closure wears the sheen
from the thread of laughter tinselling that scene.
Bell-birds pluck antiphonal notes
summoning a dream-spell halcyon and remote.

Pauline Reeve

---

*   my eternal love

Lord Jim

for Bryan Ennis

'To in the destructive element immerse'

Taut as a flagstaff, day erects itself despite
wanton sprinklers, the brazen dahlias planted for a Cup.
Just to marvel at the barricades of morning
is a kind of start before the caffeinated rush.
This is how day begins and must,
not with 'the spurious menace of wind and seas'
but a solitary purposeful figure crossing a park way too early,
not unhandsome but a freakish suit.
Repeatedly he glances over his shoulder,
framing morning's vista as if that's a rifle
oddly awkward in his pack. Rifle or tripod.
Then overtures of shadow colonise the park,
reclaim it, not even eerie yet,
unperturbed by day and its temerities.
Round the park by their windows
executives knot their ties like silky halters,
Windsored for day's slow sequacious ceremonies:
accommodations of the boardroom,
little defeats by the photocopier.
Soon I'll drive through alimentary traffic
and address those dawning boys at my old school.
But what to say after the flaccid hymn
and the gowned homily? No idea.
Breakfast is wholesome, not oratory.

Perhaps I should discourse on the romance of morning,
its bleary glory, the dahlias and detritus,
what that loping youth, glancing over his shoulder,
stooping now to light a cigarette,
discerns behind him and ahead: Lord Jim's
crazy lesson (marked *Epiphany* in red).
I'll read it to the boys from my old Penguin edition:
4/-, cracked spine, a boyish script no longer recognisable,
Peter O'Toole indestructible on the front.

Peter Rose

Love in the Precipitous City of Tea

I can't walk along the street and hail
you as I used to do. Two things have happened.
You're dead; and I haven't the walking legs.
There's a vacant way now among the ribboned
arcades where they sold goods from guns to pegs
and the mistress of the tea stall went to jail,
guilty of thieving the guns. The tipsy concertina
sang to itself, they took away the legion of the trams,
and someone even shot the barber through the glass
as he was closing shop; and how long did you live
high style with our milky waitress who married so badly
that she died in the arms of a pimp, broken like fine china?
I've gone and forgotten. It's not timetables I see,
but the tables where we clung between drunk pubs
until our eyes came round with the piping cups
and saw us back again to the same bar stool.
I only see the mistress of the tea stall
give me for nothing the gun that I shot you with,
she so loved the barber who married the love
who didn't love me, I had no money; I couldn't miss:
the barber cooking the books, and the battering pimp you
    were,
and my face of revenge exploding in the underpass,
and then this wheelchair on artificial grass
smelling of vacuum in a precipitous city that I can't see,
and, brought by our waitress, starched by custody,
a clothes peg clamping my body to its bib for tea.

David Rowbotham

We do not matter anymore

We do not matter anymore we have another night I do
not lie still my hands refuse your body your baby-rabbit
skin does not smell of anything much and when you leave
I will not even need to change the sheets there will be
nothing left but words we should not have said so quickly
so easily someone told me once to love wastefully and I
try I've tried you sleep I do not I'm up and wondering
who it might be in this wet animal heat I realise I don't
trust you half as well as I can take you on this is the
anger I need to function this is the kick I need to ache for
something for anything you'll do just fine no I can't dance
I told you but I move very well and loudly you'll learn
that I'll still be ringing in you somewhere when she's got
her lips around your accent you know I would've seen
this coming if it wasn't already happening I just got stupid
with it I've put two and two together every way that I
know how and I still come up with you and me here and
you there a woman coughs outside my window it is late
I should be all my own there should be no part of me
that is with you now up a slender thigh on a gloss-thick
mouth breathing rough-hewn words through a nasal inner
city do it do it do it baby honey sweetie I never call you
anything other than your name I thought maybe fucking
maybe mine would be enough a mouthful but still you
call me baby honey sweetie and I can't shake myself free
of the thighs you've been in I can't shake myself free of
you I want you to love me I wanna be in your liner notes
I wanna slide my tongue into the gap between your teeth
read me Celine about the kissing how we need it read it
again.

Josephine Rowe

What It Feels Like

It is two fathers punching each other in the footy sheds
shadows extending over the river flats,

over the bachelor nursing a *long neck* on his porch
over the epileptic twisting on the mechanic's floor.

It is a chorus of crows in the red gums by the river.
It is a woman avoiding loose gravel on the road to her lover.

It is the sound of water foaming up in paddocks.
It is the scrape of hoof prints on the cattle track.

It is the one finger wave above the steering wheel
a row of fox skins stretched along a fence.

a farmer growing up once his parents have died
three unmarried sisters avoiding eyes on their way out of church.

It is a gust of wind shuddering through a row of eucalypts
teenage lovers divorcing twenty years later,

my rubber boots sinking into family sayings
a man taking to his car with an axe.

Brendan Ryan

Antigone

They take away from me what they inspire
He went to what he was
For so long I represent you, a cachet
of just and true, that bones walk instead
and have to rebuild brick by brick
glorious atlas and swab, the stars, the shark sea satin'd
to become what you satirise
back to the circus and caravan
Weepy avenger coarse ground doesn't touch
– clang of sword on mattress –
I hold your fake hand to my brow
to feel love turn on and off like a program
illustrating a cliché

★

Blogs fugue into themselves,
stripping time across the shuttling lists
as music plaques over a sacked diary
and the egghead blurb's mountain of claims
and heroic tasks depicted on your shield
You know it like a bath of dirty water
How did you get stuck in that tide of boasts
and souvenirs, his royal eyes light
on the past's porphyried gas
having chucked the dolls of irony
in childhood's plastic bushes and lain path
who slab the air, obstinately
Illness drags you to the talkshows of resolve and parried death
a maypole streamers reach to, a cabinet of poison
that twins each other in dispensation for the chute

You breach the galleries' biblical catalogue and pyramid
    of sand
A tinker of song fulfils the relationship you meant to cut
trimmed and cobbled, sworn in on a whim
Rain snaps into place for myself but you, unmourned
who prepared bitterly
Thumbing a mobile, I turn from the choir

Gig Ryan

From *The Well Mouth*

Rats. Too many of them in the ship's holds
gnashing on the grain when I moved in
    saw them scattering to the corners
like dull marbles
    shooting down corridors.
Dark minds saw them come back in words
vermin under the spring
clip of this file, in
the sharp teeth
of Helvetica
    But I could see them
    this idiot-savant that I am
could count them
like spilt sticks
an eye as fast for rats
as Rainman's.

The bosses couldn't see them:
He's the sort of guy who just wants
to shit in the palace
And container ships held in port
by my too literal vision
    went floating out
like Jarlsberg cheese.

When it happens again, it's drugs.
I might consider the general humour
theory: advantage, reciprocity,
to consider the detail differently,
find some way to see the surfaces but
miss the rest.

My doctor notes my skin the blotches
          are like beetroot
          and the Indonesian islands.
And how like a counting device
my right knee clicks when I walk
how the nerves tumble down me

And the bosses and their mates and …
who else?
suggest a re-write:
that my ship comes in
when theirs goes out.

They know something that I do
not: yielding is macho
stubbornness is wet.

But I know
pedantry's a passion and no one
understands the art of it, its cult of one,
its serious attention to the facts.

The metaphysics
of staying honest.

And two men
lean on my door looking
like the same joke I have seen
but never laughed at — and speak of
Tax Department Audit. *Whistleblower*

The doctor adds condition of my stomach:
like some kind of Gothic hall
rent with rain and lightning.
                              Police
inspect my car and in a flash I could almost
admire, find rats, and drugs.
The late-night telephone calls, three seconds ECT
                              then click.
I am written out of my health
with innocent, blameless prose.

*free to listen. good or bad I hear it. they are dead. they have only
memory and the worrying through of final things. vibrations in my
water. I drift on streams. my luge and the poem underneath this pain.
I am* translating

Who am I when the cheque of me bounces?

When chemicals spill in holds or passageways
                or in the stomach late at night
under the desk lamp: the second draft
of my dissertation on unfair dismissal
takes the skin clear off my writing hand,
my face.

        And how unshakably
            it spreads,
seeing my wife and children leaving
my one-size-fits-all obsession, the awful
click in my knee as the front door closes.

Now I must for everything
see death hauled through the books.
Never thought they'd do this.

My face tight as dried varnish.
Underneath it I want to crack my
chrysalis like a hear-yee cicada

into air that's clear, into sunlight
that is sun and light that is light.

*his cargo his ship the ghost-ship one crazed man on board. the burden
of someone else's guilt turned onto him. ah yes. there was a crooked
man I knew and he had a crooked heart. I wanted to get from
underneath it too*

Where the bridge's south foundation rests
in dark suspicious mud, the Burnley tunnel's

stressing concrete to keep back, keep neutral,
things are buried, things lost from the world

of chance and sighting, of chance sighting,
are sunk. Soon – the carbon copy of my body.

Someone washing mud off their hands, the pug
stuck to the boots, how it stank and he would

never forget. Bodies buried, burnt. Our sunk
black coal. Never whistle. Honest in this worst

sense. Never sink a pot again (ironic sinking),
greet a mate or read, too closely, specifications.

Living and dead recall the smell. At the arse-end:
one looking up, one down. The buried, the burier.

Two bodies crushing down the same few images.

my skin looks like a sheet of tinfoil crushed up spread out again.
rainbows torn. is that me pissing in my own bed? are my lips still
blue? hello sailor. no I'm not the eyeful you're after. hello officer. still
walking the streets a free man instead of turning pale in prison? I can
hear you so you must be safe. in hell

Philip Salom

Flying Through Glass

Given the state of the garden
weeds choking the rose
even the Hill's Volvo
never could guess
if the wings of this duckling
sewn with thorn and bone
would aim like a swan
at the moon over Gordon
thrown like a tennis ball
caught from a courtly past
hailed from a cage
in the deep of the glass
now my down, now my feathers,
gone last year's Christmas roast
under the trapped life
sings a wild brindle dog.

Winifred Sanderson

An Awful Wedding

John Clare married Madness in the garden
and she was beautiful.
The birds hopped around them on the damp
ground under the oaks
the sparrows, finches and robins
wagged their heads.
It was a weird cold day in high summer,
the day of the wedding.
Did she feel cruel
marrying such a one as this?
Such a fine poet.

Under the green of the trees he
looked only fourteen
and held her hand so tightly
for fear of being abandoned:
left to walk
the fields and elm copses under low dark cumuli
fearful of falling into deep mill streams
where only trout would heed him.

She did not want to leave him alone
swaying love-lost under nights,
transfixed by the rise of a single star.
How could she?
He had fallen in love with something too great
and she had found him in the nick of time,
trembling, all tangled under blackberries.

His pastoral poems, had taken flight as birds
and jeered at him from high roosts.

So shy, he looks at her loveliness and knows
he has found a safe haven from all the waste
the wild surplus of the garden.
Sometimes he cold not
bear it. The way the light ran
riotous through the woods on a windy day
was enough to make him weep.

She will be the provider. You can see it in
the strength of her plump arms wrapt around his hips.
When he is weary again she will be waiting.
Ever faithful. Ever frightful.

Kirsty Sangster

Mr Habitat on Anger

So many bastards. Right? All inconsiderate.
Like a teacher, new to a rough area school,
who has his patience stretched and stretched

to see at what extreme self-control
will finally snap, I am target.
For safety's sake, I won't crack. Keep track

of my volcano with a mental seismograph.
Take anger out of four-walled limits
at a rapid pace into open space, and know

what it is to be released, genetically,
into a world of scheming beasts. I circumvent
criminal intent, but anger doesn't

suss it – shivers the leaves
of the sycamore trees. Goes it alone.
Darkly: there are no paths or poems

within the cerebellum. Or police. But terrific range.
And fear, anger's fuel, enough to create
an urgent look as of a man on day release.

Andrew Sant

In the Neck

Old Transylvania! Folklore and horror schlock
sauntering down the aisle, fingers deliciously
entwined. Midnight, French windows, curtains
blowing, the heroine asleep – some hoping
for a miracle, most of us hot for the vampire.
Back then, when evil was pure black & white,
and blood trickled black as ink. When sex
and fear held hands, leaving it at that.

Odd to remember now, kissing her on the neck –
all first-love awkwardness, all sudden pink
confusion. First love? Now there's a vampire
to leave a window open for, happy to be
sprung. Discerning bat, swooping only
through the casements of the young.

Michael Sariban

Cicadas

Cicadas outside. How fragile is our security.
I think of the Canadian lakes without frogs
I remember Christmas Beetles this time of year.
The humidity at night is right. Memory
Pulls at the strings, but the beetles do not come.
All these years underground, learning their process:
Are the cicadas going to continue the cycle?
We have come to expect the inevitable silence.

You said, do we have anything to talk about
Any more? I held my tongue, conscious
Of the way speech requires exertion from the mouth
Taken for granted until it is no longer automatic.
If we find the cicada shells outside stuck
To some convenient bush or rail, will we rejoice?

Thomas Shapcott

Lucky for Some
(What the Soothsayer Said)

You have been born in a place and a time and with skin
that you'd never have chosen;

you are the mirror's dark side and its front
that reflects other people's opinions;

urchins will call out what you are and laugh
when you walk in the streets of strange cities.

Some people, hearing your name, will suppose you have died.
You will be alien no matter what land you live in.

When people meet and you're present, they will not see you.
You will see houses and tombs of your forebears erased.

You will wake each morning knowing no thought is your own
and you'll be free to die of shame.

When you think of 'being', you'll hear spiders chewing flies.
You'll never know the child you were.

You'll find it's lonesome being you.
Your siblings will keep lists of your betrayals.

Those you come to think of as your friends will not recall
what you have lent them or a word that you have said.

You'll work for those who make the task of waking up
a nightmare each day.

You'll find excuses when the widows and the widowers
of those you call your friends invite you in. They'll hate you
  more.

You'll live to be a connoisseur of coffins and regret
that you've seen better than the ones of those you love.

Women of such beauty that you can't believe it's true
will chop your heart to sausage mince

and tie themselves to worthless men.
You'll have a long life to remember all of this.

When you write, your ears will be torn off and nailed to
  doors
so that the world can have a place to pour its filth.

Your eyes will fill with broken limbs like trees smashed in a
  gale;
there'll be no time for talk of love.

Your children who are soft as grass before the reaper's blade
have been corrupted while we speak.

Not because you put your trust in words,
for what it's worth, a poem, please.

Michael Sharkey

Break Up

An artist's land is only walls,
yet her hands were like a farmer's hands,
worked up, a size too big for her body.
Her studio was a field and gym
where skin lines opened up like cuts
and all colours mixed to grasses and muds
graining her fingers with miniature tracks.

The day we settled our affairs
her swelled skunned knuckle was healing
to purple, her fingernails were long closed eyelids,
under each were lashes of grime
as if it might indeed be soil
she works with, some peasant manual way
of harrowing earth in plots of masonite squares,
her grip strong as mine, arms lean, vein-vined
as she took my hand for one last time
but to shake like two men, staring, without kissing.

Craig Sherborne

Ash Saturday

There is no God, I was made in *this* man's image:
those slate-dark eyes of his are mine,
the dented bridge of our his-my nose.
I laugh with his rasping cackle in me.
I walk with his stooping, trudging gait,
swearing his 'Jesus bloody Christ'
in a sudden fist-curl of temper.
My right ear points like a flesh-antenna as his does,
and being my father I bear his name.
Haphazardries of kin passed on from birth
that to see him wizened on his cancer bed,
his insides turned to water,
is to view my own death, my own Dorian Gray
smiling, weeping in the drug-bliss of sleeping
or counting out life on his fingers:
'I've got more money than I thought,' he says.
'And I can't even wipe my arse.'
I soak a flannel and do it for him,
the first time I've touched his privates.
The doctor says he could go on for hours,
but no he won't, the nurse assures me.
She gives him a last injection.
'If there's something unsaid, best say it now.
He won't wake up from this one.'

Now I scatter him in the surf.
This is what a man burns down to:
bone's grey grit like broken pebbles.

Not ash but grit and blood-brown dust
from the coffin they called 'Mahogany'.
The same salt 'n' pepper as his shaven stubble
that whiskered the sink-white from his razor,
the Brylcreemed hair he palmed skin-smooth
after combing with his tongue poked forward.
Some of him sticks to my swimming hands—
I shudder and dunk to wash him from me,
splash myself like an accidental ritual,
but it's too late, the symbol remains:
He always stood between me and death,
but now I'm next in line, I inherit his future,
a law bequeathed that's impossible to alter,
a murder-chain sanctioned as natural.

I've already moved into his death:
I've tried on his clothes for a decent fit
and sorted the rest for the Salvos.
I used his screwdriver to jemmy the plug
from this beige plastic tube he came in.
It exhaled a false puff of breath.
In a minute I'll escort my mother from the beach,
her taking my arm like a younger he,
casting his funeral flowers to the shallows.
'Looks cold that water,' she'll worry with a shiver.
'You don't think we should have buried him?'
She'll complain how the pins-and-needles sand
is stinging her legs like mosquitoes.

She'll hope out loud there's nothing funny with his will
and expects her sister to be over for a hand-out.
Then we'll turn for one more chance to watch
where his slick dissolved in the buckled swell,
stretched into invisibility.
I'll blink and utter 'Goodness' with her
as if death really was a mystery after all
and dwells out there in all that sea and twilight.
But death's no mystery, not to me, not now.
I am its DNA.

Craig Sherborne

Boy

The rough and tumble of the schoolyard
is always welcome relief from a room
papered with whispers, where every night

he must taste the salted honey of his pain
or else listen to the chorus of lies
that they hiss to one another in the dark.

When he can't get to sleep in such dark
he gazes at where he knows the backyard
ends in a clump of wisteria – there lies

his secret, there he can shelter from his room
and pretend to escape from the pain
and pretend he isn't trembling in the night.

And he does tremble, if not every night
then at least when the inflexions of the dark
and the hissed whispers and the pain

cause him for moments to forget the yard
and listen again to the echoes that the room
so magnifies and all those ceaseless lies.

At school of course everybody lies
but brazenly, not in whispers like the night
or the bittersweet aloneness of the room

or the limpid coruscations of the dark –
it is different in the bazaar of the schoolyard
where shouts conceal the words for pain.

The wisteria grove is his refuge, no pain
can reach him there, and all the lies
melt away in that magical backyard

corner he stares into from the heart of night
where he can tangle himself inside a dark
of stubborn branches, and there is always room

for the honey of silence inside and room
for the shedding of his fear and his pain
and in those shadows he is sheltered from dark

as he sits entwined in the wisteria or he lies
prone and nuzzles to the grass until night
is ready to descend and he must leave the yard.

Must return to his room, where he lies
in his five-year-old pain, waiting for night
to end and for dark to give back his backyard.

Alex Skovron

Cold Was the Ground

dark was the night
Blind Willie Johnson huffs in my ears
weeping into God. How easy to loop
the past into a soundtrack, light digestion
& here's Willie, scratching life into the air
carving out sight & sense in the squall
So many spills, paths of only one take
So simple, the hatching of intrigue &
sloppy way we invent moments to be sad
I walk at the trees as if I have knowledge
secrets of their past, I don't, but confidence
is a clever accessory. This winter walk
these minuets stall the loud, awaken the soft
my ears, warm with the blues
my eyes with the slow mountain
& the snow, suspended in a mid-fall spill
whitening out everything that came before

alicia sometimes

Fire

This fire is a terrible mistake
I think as I step in
I am rising from it
my eyes terrified
and I see below
your body of flame
Only seek I thought
and I must find the light
and yet its phosphorescent glory
burns all for miles before it
and all the world is a fire
and the things of man
are boxes to deposit
the charred remains
I am ash in your office tower
ground bone in your mercedes
my teeth fall like pearls
into the cuffs of your trousers
I am vapour in your library
a rose on your coffee table
my silver plaque hangs
All the world is a blaze
and you lie crucified upon it
and raise your hands
like tongues of fire
and I know it is a mistake
to reach my hand into your pain
that burns in me
telling me I will be purified
so I step in again
into the circle of flame.

Kathleen Stewart

Night by Night

Strawberries ripen by the back door.
Rain patterns a pond's surface
and fills the fountain to overflowing.

The fish hid for two weeks, we assumed
an egret or kookaburra had removed them
the way a surgeon removes cancer.

Rain falls with vertical precision.
Someone appeared last night at the gate
to the park, appeared and was gone again.

No wind. They rise strawberry red
under the pond's surface
which dimples where their mouths touch air.

What did she want? If I wait beside the pond
in the rain till 3 a.m. will she come again
to the park gate? This geometry

of perpendicular rain is ruffled
by a rising breeze. Is it her passing
that is stirring the leaves? The surgeon

has finished his work and the body's labour begins.
Strawberries hang by the back door
and rain for a moment hides as the fish hid.

She will come again at 3, I know it
the way a shoulder presages rain.
3 a.m. By the gate leading to the dark park.

Andrew Taylor

Dentist's Waiting Room

Flicking through the mags checking the tsunami diet,
the asylum seeker's boob job and Terri Schiavo's horoscope,
I asked myself, 'If Camilla can become Princess of Wales,
why can't Shane Warne be the next Pope?'
It would, of course, be more in keeping with tradition
if those roles were reversed, but let's not think too deeply
about such weighty matters; let's instead
amuse our winter selves with poolside skimming
through the glossy travel supplement of *Island*
imagining those cute poems with little umbrellas over them.
When *Ten Days of Ten Eighty* comes along I know it's time
to head for the intellectual stimulus of Port Douglas.
Pass the *history wars* brand sunblock and my
Reconciliation sarong, the green one.

But before I go, a quick cap and polish;
when I smile, wide as a thylacine, I want
to be described as photogenic.

Tim Thorne

Girl in Water

Waiting to meet a pretty girl – any pretty girl –
hot summer day in 1958, beach crowd, emotional algebra,
also list and remember: makeup, perfume, lipstick, talc,
telephone passion – no, a soda fountain, a pizza.

Do they dream of mystery and adventure, women?
or do girls want to drown in literature? No, stupid. I
bet she'd like a fragrant pizza topped with mozzarella,
or is that just me? A movie: Item: Kim Novak. A drive-in –

yes, more subtle and powerful appetites litter the sand.
So become that detective, wounded, pitiful; so
learn to love and learn to fall in love, in the back row at the
    Bijou,
in parked cars, or snug among sandhills ... your spyglass a nib,

keyhole secrets memorised and filed away, until
eternity comes calling at the foot of a staircase.
After that ending, another climb, another cliff
beyond which something awful awaits: love

or falling in love or into love or falling into death, a
uniform and dizzying and swift descent
that leaves you breathless, leaves you
very unsteady like a cork in the water,

effervescent and febrile and emotionally labile,
ready for almost anything.
That conscious pilot spoke: *scripsi quod scripsi*:
I have written what? I have written for

girl in water 'girl in water', girl
or woman in waves of water. I
keen to find behind mirrors, wavering echoes, burn
in plots and complex narratives to draw

many clues out, threads of meaning. A
new insight into the convoluted plot
of good and evil I can look for, where good men whine,
villains struggle to prevail and bluster

against ordinary background noise and hubbub:
kaleidoscopes of criminality and subtle fiscal judo
scam and prosper, and some ordinary guy
will win and lose everything. I

owe more than money. The key will turn:
nervous ex-detectives afraid of causing harm
drop into floods of anxiety, plunge into semi-
enervating doubt; whirlpools of suspicion, and later

refuse help from well-meaning friends or
from glum old girl-friends, dawdling, doodling, who
understand too well their weaknesses, their
lack of manly self-respect, who know how hypnotic

those doubled mysteries within a mystery are. You reach
into a maelstrom of neurosis. Beyond bodily desire,
these complex chess-like fantasies are the true romantic
scenes in your life: the most ludic acrostic paradises: click!

John Tranter

running with knives
on a slippery surface

insanity doesn't run in my family,
he walks slowly, and carries a big stick.

he takes me to the park of familiar noises and
spins me too fast on the merry-go-round.
he takes me walking through minefields in clown shoes
with my little red wagon, collecting victims and empties
and things that go thump in the night.
he takes me stalking the corners of a lifestyle that
no amount of pretending or latex will ever let me join in.
he takes me running with knives on a slippery surface.
he takes me.

he leaves me wrapped up in costumes, too afraid
to get naked.
he leaves me blessed with a vicious beauty, making
me feel more manatee than mermaid.
he leaves me confusing my muse with an addictive
    personality,
spitting distance from reality but it's all done
with smoke and mirrors.
he leaves me seeing my fears in double vision.
he leaves me.

he drags me along in the hand of illusion, cold hands
for good or evil.
he drags me (kicking and screaming) down the aisle
to my permanent pew in the chapel of unrequited love.
he drags me to the roof and makes me dizzy.
he drags me under the riptide, where it's darker than
a month of new moon midnites, not waving, not drowning,
not even really treading water.
he drags me under.

insanity doesn't run.

Kerryn Tredrea

Four Apocalyptic Quatrains: The Australian Wheat Board–Iraq Bribery Scandal

The call of the strange bird is heard
on the pipe of the breathing floor;
so high will become the bushels of wheat
that man will cannibalise his fellow man ...
—Nostradamus, Quatrain 75 (c. 1568)

We learn, yet forget, in the cataclysm of our birth
the owl songs of Muk Muk;
the death feather, reacquainted we will be again
in the sunset of our mortality.
(The call of the strange bird is heard ...)

The dijeridoo sits in the corner of my room
near the window, ghosts breathe
my frailty of spirit
resonates in the acoustics of this gouged plain.
(... on the pipe of the breathing floor ...)

The dark skin ripped apart
perished dreams of the Dreamtime
to the new crops of the Invader;
blood furrows this occupied soil of neo-pestilence.
(... so high will become the bushels of wheat ...)

Harvested by the demon-seed of the Invader
and grain fed to the insatiable hunger
of the Dictator, red-handed
the hands bite the hands that have fed them.
(... that man will cannibalise his fellow man ...)

Sam Wagan Watson

Prologue from *The Universe Looks Down*

Milena is a scribe. She turns to the tabula rasa
And squints down at that snowblank sheet of paper.
She takes up a pen. Writes the first word.
Is this the very root of consciousness?
Not so. How did she know paper and pen,
How this concept of making a mark, and then
Where is any possible tabula rasa?

She tries again, noticing that she thinks
And no necromancer can quarrel with that;
But where did she get this very notion of thinking?
But for the word she could swim in pure consciousness
Or a fiat of God ...
            You might go barmy,
These doubts advancing over you like an army.
A cup of tea and a scone, Milena thinks,

Will calm her nerves and go with a good sit down.
Milena appears both dutiful and beautiful,
An enviable blend, surely.
She is the type who wouldn't rage off on a quest,
She is the type who sits here in control:
More will emerge about her role
As we trace divergent destinies on down

Or out, into whatever is meant by Fate.
(By loss of memory we are reborn
But memory is the active root of power.)
A sparrow scuffles on the windowsill
Like the germ of Pure Idea dropping in
So that a narrative can begin:
When set in motion, folk engender fate.

But fate has meaning only in a frame.
Could there be a destiny of mountains
Or something tragic happening to a gene?
We sketch clear selves against a universe
We do not really know at all
Nor why there should be selves that rise and fall
Nor where to hang our tidy little frame.

The screen of reality gave way to change
Quick as a switchflip. Desert carpeted,
Horizon walled about, this all was something else.
Another age unlocked its train of rulers:
In suits of blue or desolate grey,
Desolate armour to keep reality away.
The heart of power is it has to change.

The first was portly and articulate
Brooding over cricket or the old Cinque Ports;
He read the country when he needed to,
Spinning perceptions into rhetoric.
Now his enormous bottom swayed on past
As though he were Queen Victoria at last,
Utterly angloid and articulate.

Next was a man reformed, and therefore dour,
Who took on the traumata of a war
And turned our faces east toward Brobdingnag
With its inexhaustible guns and showering bombs
– 'our?' Grab the microphone, like noise Norman Mailer.
The truly strong will reinvent Australia
With miles of sheep and shiraz for their dower.

She knows who butters her bread,
Or should do, seeing she grew the grain,
But now sits back to watch the pooh-bahs pass:
The modest engine driver at his pipe,
One left inside the belly of a shark.
The twerp who came next barely left a mark.
And then emerged a giant of a different breed,

His thronged supporters chanting that 'It's time,'
And so it was, but soon enough
The screen of reality gave way to change:
The fabric of his governance was unravelled
By another longshanks, an Easter Island squatter
Who later came to sing a different tune.
Were all of them only reaching for the moon?
There is so little we can do in time,

Our liquid medium, our joy and curse,
In faces and in mirrors for ever trickling,
As Hofmannsthal complained: the man who wrote
That baffled cry, the 'Letter of Lord Chandos'.
Art gives both flow and stillness like our fountains
Yet we're plain trivial compared to mountains,
With consciousness our curse.

Now that the wheel has turned, we can
Put a collection of static shots together:
The bleach-haired larrikin; the sly
Boy from Bankstown in his fancy suits;
And little Giglamps with his mania for
Pushing the country into some useful war –
Earnest diggers will always carry the can

But this is only Nation. My bright stage
Is the world, or else the universe,
In which we can dismantle clockwork time.
Tantara, trumpets! Swing it, saxophones!
We'll have the tinsel and the strobe lights next,
Greasepaint is daubed, and properties are fixed.
We're playing this upon the open stage.

Milena is almost secular. So am I.
We watch the figures of our yearning tramp
Across their stages, differently endowed
With different hungers, ready-made ideals,
As well as with a personal DNA
And all that means. I say, I say, I say …
There's more to identity than meets the eye.

Chris Wallace-Crabbe

Sister

Her axolotl dips in his cage of water,
his polite uneraseable smile swanning
him upward, the rubbery, tail-heavy dragon's
body tilting downward. The tiny golden
Aztec eyes, blind, lidlessly slumber through the dim
waters of the kitchen aquarium,
like never-quite-sinking coins, or beacons adrift
with scarcely the ghost of a reference

to the mythical flicker of the salamander
he genetically sidesteps, even surpasses
by his own more modern brand of indestructible
– his species kept alive by scientists
for its ability to regenerate:
his limbs, if lost, will soon resprout; even
some parts of the brain, if chewed off by
a sibling, grow back. Only the crude lungs

connect him to a world outside him;
once a day he noses the surface and breathes –
then free-falls back down into depths
of swirling grit. Ever larval, babyish red ragged
gills fronding wildly round a blunt head,
sealed by water in the jewel of himself,
he survived the pumping of his stomach
after gutsing seven lumps of gravel.

Descendant of the Aztec dog-god,
Xolotl, who with mangled hands and feet
guided the dead to heaven, his once trans-
lucent form refuses catastrophe. More
than the ailing tabby, the timorous
and watchful high-heeled dog or the fire-
prone house, he guards our dangerous
childhood pledge to never change.

Petra White

Riverina Weather Report

This is a catalogue of prayer
in the company of brawling possums
tossed black Saturday night
with a searchlight moon engraved with curses
& growls of freight trains heading north.
I think about us.

Like the furry clash on tin
our choices are inescapable
each rimed with peril
with its roots in a loam of convenience.
This winter has lurched up
like half-dead livestock.
Rain is a miser's smear
of hope over odds.

Will it happen for us
our new bridges of silence
the paddock gates we close, lock
with corroded chain
& hand-shaped latches?
We are promised some kind of haven
but without fodder.

To aspire to the life of smaller birds,
the gold clamour of wings as they flit amongst
smudged olive leaf & incandescent lillipilli berries.
I will try again
on the next return. League's Club dinner
& three glasses of champagne. The affirmation of our fingertips,
habit of our hearts.

Les Wicks

Station blue

from under the door of the railway toilets blue ekes out
like old disco like the suggestion of a *close encounter*
I ask someone they say it's so you can't find the vein
to stick the needle in
the mirror inside shows my face bones dressed in a sick skin
but it is a trick of the light I am well my arms trackless
heart beat you could set time by
visitor from the country clean white alien
washing the blue from her hands

Jane Williams

The Kingsbury Tales: the scholar's tale

The scholar, mostly a quiet man, with a large head, I think,
    of history
Erupted last night in a lunch party that lasted seven hours
    from midday
And that showed no sign of ending
At the mention of the Japanese massacre in Nanjing:

It's not just in Nanjing
But in Dalian, in Tianjin, in Lüshun, and in many other
    Chinese cities
The Japs carried out their atrocities
The Japanese have to be killed, if you are a Chinese, you
    know this, they have to!

I took another look at him this time but I saw the same
    person
The scorching words did not seem to touch anyone else
My friends kept eating drinking talking, one even
    commenting on
How nice my Italian leather shoes of a chestnut colour looked

I know the scholar's tale without him talking
Gained his Ph.D in Hong Kong and drifted downwards in
    Melbourne
Till he was out of employment permanently
Staying at the bottom teaching Chinese and history to
    primary/secondary students

But he is a good drinker of whisky and occasionally when he
    wants
He tells a good story, too, for, afterwards, in a quieter
    moment
He tells me that I am a real hooligan because I subvert the
    Chinese language
Something he cannot but worship whereas he is not one in
    the truest sense of the word

Even though, years ago, he, with his gang of four,
    encountered a gang of thirty
In an iron mining that he had been sent to during the
    Cultural Revolution
And he took the lead in the charge. With his axe, he took
    hold of the guy
From the enemy gang and hacked him to near death, the
    guy's head covered in blood

Facing us is another scholar, from Sydney, who had raised the
    issue of hooliganism
He smiled and said nothing, apparently unimpressed with
    either him or me
Indulging in his own memory of having supervised a Chinese
    Ph.D to success
With a thesis on literary hooligans, written in Chinese, in
    Sydney

Ouyang Yu

Publication Details

Bruce Beaver's 'Prelude' and 'On Re-Reading Amis, Wain and Larkin' appeared in *The Long Game*, University of Queensland Press, St Lucia, 2005.

Shelton Lea's 'Nebuchadnezzar' appeared in *Nebuchadenezzar*, Black Pepper, North Fitzroy, 2005.

Richard Deutch's 'Danger' appeared in *After Words*, Wild and Woolley, Watsons Bay, 2005.

Vera Newsome's 'Midnight' and 'Matins, 1932' will appear in the forthcoming anthology *Gratia,* Five Islands Press, Carlton, 2006.

Lisa Bellear's 'To No One: And Mary Did Time' appeared on the *Australia – Poetry International* website, 2006.

Robert Adamson's 'A Visitation' appeared in the *Australian*, 31 December 2005.

Judith Beveridge's 'Jellyfish' appeared in *Getting it Right, Heat 10* (new series), edited by Ivor Indyk, Giramondo, 2005; and 'Lingo' appeared in the 2006 Broadway Poetry Prize anthology.

Judith Bishop's 'Still Life with Cockles and Shells' appeared in *Australian Book Review*, March 2006.

Ken Bolton's 'Coffee' appeared in *At the Flash & At the Baci*, Wakefield Press, Kent Town, 2006.

Peter Boyle's '20/5/04' appeared in *Blast: Poetry and Other Critical Writing*, no. 2, September 2005.

David Brooks' 'One Hundred Nights' appeared in *Walking to Point Clear: Poems 1983–2002*, Brandl & Schlesinger Poetry, 2005.

Kevin Brophy's 'A Dictionary of Sentences' appeared in *Wet Ink*, no. 2, Autumn 2006.

Pam Brown's 'To a City' appeared in the *Age*.

James Charlton's 'Letter to Walt Whitman re Iraq' appeared in the *Age*, 12 August 2006.

Aidan Coleman's 'Blue-Tongue' appeared in *Avenues & Runways*, Brandl & Schlesinger Poetry, 2005.

MTC Cronin's 'Foxglove' appeared in *The Flower, The Thing*, University of Queensland Press, St Lucia, 2006.

Bruce Dawe's 'Why Liberation from Dictatorship May Take Some Time' appeared in the *Australian*, 14–15 January 2006.

Rosemary Dobson's 'Divining Colander' appeared in *Australian Book Review*, June–July 2006.

Laurie Duggan's 'Fantasia on a Theme by T.S. Eliot' appeared in *The Passenger*, University of Queensland Press, St Lucia, 2006.

Stephen Edgar's 'Golden Coast' appeared in *Space: New Writing*, no. 3, eds Anthony Lynch and David McCooey, Whitmore Press, Geelong, Victoria, 2006.

Diane Fahey's 'The Ibis Grove' appeared in the *Sea Wall and River Light*, Five Islands Press, Carlton, 2006.

Michael Farrell's 'bagboy' appeared in the *Age*, 14 January 2006.

Barbara Fisher's 'The Poet's Sister' appeared in *Southerly,* vol. 66, no. 1, Winter 2006.

Cameron Fuller's 'A Relationship with Fear' appeared in *Friendly Street New Poets 11*, Friendly Street Poets Inc. in association with Wakefield Press, Kent Town, 2006.

Kevin Gillam's 'chair pose' appeared in *Meanjin*, vol. 65, no. 1, 2006.

Ross Gillett's 'In Praise of Mania' appeared in *The Sea Factory*, New Poets Series XI, Five Islands Press, Carlton, 2006.

Alan Gould's 'In Thought They Lived like Russians' appeared in *Quadrant*, December 2005.

Jamie Grant's 'Fireplace' appeared in *Quadrant*, January–February 2006.

Jeff Guess's 'Somewhere on the Shelves' appeared in *Westerly*.

Susan Hampton's *The Kindly Ones* was published by Five Islands Press, Carlton, 2005.

Jennifer Harrison's 'Hand, Chainsaw and Head' and 'Changzhuo's Bees' appeared in *Folly & Grief*, Black Pepper, North Fitzroy, 2006.

J.S. Harry's 'West of Al Shualla' appeared in *Australian Book Review*, September 2005.

Susan Hawthorne's 'Strange Tractors' appeared in *The Butterfly Effect*, Spinifex Press, Melbourne, 2005.

Nguyen Tien Hoang's 'They' appeared in the *Age*, 25 February 2006.

Clive James's 'Double or Quits' appeared in the *Australian*, 22 July 2006.

John Jenkins' 'The Library in the Snow' appeared in *Blue Dog*, vol. 4, no. 8, Poetry Australia Foundation Inc., November 2005.

Judy Johnson's 'The Photographer Francis Bacon and Sylvia Plath Stalk Big Game in Equatorial Africa' appeared in *Blue Dog*, vol. 5, no. 9, June 2006.

Jill Jones's 'Waking Alone by the Radio' appeared in *Space: New Writing,* no. 3, eds Anthony Lynch and David McCooey, Whitmore Press, Geelong, Victoria, 2006.

Jean Kent's 'A Luminous Tortoise Near Muswellbrook' appeared in *Sheltered Lives, HEAT 11,* (new series), edited by Ivor Indyk, Giramondo, Sydney, 2006.

John Kinsella's 'Reflectors: Drive 5, Part 1' appeared in *The New Arcadia*, Fremantle Arts Centre Press, Fremantle, 2005.

Andy Kissane's 'Happiness' appeared in *Island*, no. 103, Summer 2005.

Andrew Lansdown's 'Prayer' appeared in *Quadrant*, May 2006.

Anthony Lawrence's 'Stingers' appeared in *Space: New Writing*, no. 3, eds Anthony Lynch and David McCooey, Whitmore Press, Geelong, Victoria, 2006.

Josef Lesser's 'live crab a la cordon bleu a la S' appeared in *Five Bells*, Spring 2005.

Emma Lew's 'Luminous Alias' appeared in *Star Dust, HEAT 9*, (new series), edited by Ivor Indyk, Giramondo, Sydney, 2005.

Yve Louis' 'The Wedding' appeared in *The Yellow Dress*, Five Islands Press, Carlton, 2005.

Jennifer Maiden's 'Together We Will a Cheese Achieve' and 'Foxfall 1, 2, 3' appeared in *Friendly Fire*, Giramondo, Sydney, 2005.

Annette Marner's 'Midnight Drive' appeared in *Women With Their Faces On Fire*, Friendly Street Poets, Wakefield Press, Kent Town, 2006.

Ian McBryde's 'Songs for Paul' will appear in *The Adoption Order*, Five Islands Press, Carlton, 2006.

Shane McCauley's 'Entropy' appeared in *Glassmaker*, Sunline Press, Cottesloe, 2005.

Mal McKimmie's 'Jubilate Anger' appeared in *Blast*, vol. 3, 2006.

Graeme Miles' 'Some Things the Body Knows' appeared in *Phosphorescence*, Fremantle Arts Centre Press, Fremantle, 2006.

John Millett's 'Street Preacher – Surfers Paradise' and 'Widows at Jupiter's Casino' appeared in *The People Singers: The Surfers Paradise Poems*, Five Islands Press, Carlton, 2005.

Peter Minter's 'Voyager' appeared in *Blue Grass*, Salt Publishing, Cambridge, UK, 2006.

Stephen Muecke's 'Post Orientalism' appeared in *Meanjin*, vol. 64, no. 4. 2005.

Les Murray's 'The Nostril Songs' appeared in *The Biplane Houses*, Black Inc., Melbourne, 2006.

Jan Owen's 'Horizon' appeared in *Friendly Street Poets Thirty*, eds. Rob Walker and Louise Nicholas, Friendly Street Poets Inc. in association with Wakefield Press, 2006.

Neil Paech's *beached rd* was published by Wakefield Press, Kent Town, 2006.

Geoff Page's *Freehold* was published by Brandl & Schlesinger Poetry, 2005.

K.F. Pearson's 'His Literary Reputation' appeared in *The Apparition at Large*, Black Pepper, North Fitzroy, 2006.

Pauline Reeve's 'Sugarloaf Sequence' will appear in *Blue Dog*, no. 10, October 2006.

Peter Rose's 'Lord Jim' appeared in *Australian Book Review*, June–July 2006.

David Rowbotham's 'Love in the Precipitous City of Tea' appeared in *The Cave in the Sky*, Picaro Press, Warners Bay, 2005.

Brendan Ryan's 'What It Feels Like' appeared in *Australian Book Review*, February 2006.

Gig Ryan's 'Antigone' appeared in *Star Dust, HEAT 9*, (new series), edited by Ivor Indyk, Giramondo, Sydney, 2005.

Philip Salom's *The Well Mouth* was published by Fremantle Arts Centre Press, Fremantle, 2005.

Kirsty Sangster's 'An Awful Wedding' appeared in *Midden Places*, Black Pepper, North Fitzroy, 2006.

Andrew Sant's 'Mr Habitat on Anger' appeared in the *Weekend Australian*.

Thomas Shapcott's 'Cicadas' appeared in the *Weekend Australian*, 1–2 July 2006.

Michael Sharkey's 'Lucky for Some (What the Soothsayer Said)' appeared in *LiNQ*, vol. 33, 2006.

Craig Sherborne's 'Break Up' and 'Ash Saturday' appeared in *Necessary Evil*, Black Inc., Melbourne, 2006.

Alex Skovron's 'Boy' appeared in *Australian Book Review*, March 2006.

alicia sometimes' 'Cold was the Ground' appeared in the *Age*, 26 November 2005.

Andrew Taylor's 'Night by Night' appeared in *Sheltered Lives, HEAT 11,* (new series), edited by Ivor Indyk, Giramondo, Sydney, 2006.

Tim Thorne's 'Dentist's Waiting Room' appeared in the *Age*, 10 September 2005.

John Tranter's 'Girl in Water' appeared in *Urban Myths: 210 Poems*, University of Queensland Press, St Lucia, 2006.

Kerryn Tredrea's 'running with knives on a slippery surface' appeared in *Friendly Street Poets Thirty*, eds. Rob Walker and Louise Nicholas, Friendly Street Poets Inc. in association with Wakefield Press, 2006.

Samuel Wagan Watson's 'Four Apocalyptic Quatrains' appeared in *Meanjin*, vol. 65, no. 1, 2006.

Chris Wallace-Crabbe's *The Universe Looks Down* was published by Brandl & Schlesinger Poetry, 2005.

Les Wicks' 'Riverina Weather Report' appeared in *Blue Dog*.

Jane Williams' 'Station blue' appeared in *The Last Tourist*, Five Islands Press, Carlton, 2006.

Ouyang Yu's 'The Kingsbury Tales: the scholar's tale' appeared in *Griffith REVIEW 10: Family Politics*, ABC Books, Summer 2005–2006, <www.griffith.edu.au/griffithreview>.